praise for

i'm not yelling

"Elizabeth Leiba is the voice first-generation Caribbean immigrant professional women have been patiently waiting for!! She has answers for the overachievers who are scared to ask questions because they are expected to have all the answers. Whew, this one hits different! Everyone talks about authenticity, but Elizabeth is showing how using your authentic voice and ditching the code-switching can be a path to freedom and achievement. I AM YELLING, LOL—IF YOU NEED A SIGN TO READ THE BOOK, HERE IT IS!"

—**Sue-Ann Robinson**, Esq., lead counsel for Ben Crump Law in Ft. Lauderdale

"Leiba's work is a strategic tool for Black women navigating corporate America and their allies working to create supportive environments. *I'm Not Yelling* is the guide you mark with highlights and get out of your purse at work to address difficult conversations. It's the literary sister circle you need to find the strength to get back up on the days you feel unsupported and alone."

—**Qaadirah Abdur-Rahim**, chief equity officer, City of Atlanta

"What a gift to Black women in the workplace! Leiba's work elevates and amplifies a conversation that is long overdue. With fierce, unapologetic vulnerability, Leiba unpacks the complexity and nuance of this sometimes-debilitating trope impacting so many Black women. For those committed to challenging stereotypes and enhancing workplace inclusion, this book is a must read."

—**Dana Brownlee**, *Forbes* careers senior contributor

"In *I'm Not Yelling*, Elizabeth Leiba sheds light on some of the common, and troubling, challenges Black women face in the workplace. She offers actionable steps that we, as Black women, can take to beat the odds stacked against us. This guide will support us in obtaining long-term success and peace."

—**Aiko Bethea, Esq.**, author and founder of RARE Coaching & Consulting

i'm not yelling

i'm not yelling

yelling

A Black Woman's
Guide to Navigating
the Workplace

**ELIZABETH
LEIBA**

mango
PUBLISHING

CORAL GABLES

For permission requests, please contact the publisher at:
Mango Publishing Group
2850 S Douglas Road, 4th Floor
Coral Gables, FL 33134 USA
info@mango.bz

For special orders, quantity sales, course adoptions and corporate sales, please email the publisher at sales@mango.bz. For trade and wholesale sales, please contact Ingram Publisher Services at customer.service@ingramcontent.com or +1.800.509.4887.

I'm Not Yelling: A Black Woman's Guide to Navigating the Workplace

Library of Congress Cataloging-in-Publication number: 2022913384
ISBN: (p) 978-1-68481-073-4 (e) 978-1-68481-074-1
BISAC category code: BUS009000, BUSINESS & ECONOMICS / Business Etiquette

contents

foreword

"**W**hy are you yelling?"

As a Black woman, I have had those words hurled at me more times than I care to remember. Most of us have. They are on page one of the "Angry Black Woman Trope" manual. They are usually accusatory, spoken by someone who does not look like us.

The subtext of this phrase, informed by history and epigenetics, is: "Who do you think you are?" "Why are you holding your ground?" "Why are you holding me accountable?" "Why aren't you letting me control you?"

"How. Dare. You. Be. Uppity." And the N-word is silent.

This phrase is weaponized to police our tone. It is an attempt to manipulate us into quiet submission. It is meant to mute our voice.

The thing is, I was never yelling. **We** were never yelling. I was merely speaking my truth—calmly—and staying grounded in my principles.

Admittedly, there was a time when I might have allowed myself to be bullied into speechlessness. Those days have gone. I refuse to be silenced. **We** refuse to be silenced. And we know that we do not have to yell in order to make our voices heard.

There is a famous saying:

"When you're accustomed to privilege, equality feels like oppression."

—Unknown

I would proffer this version for addition to the lexicon:

*"When your peace is predicated on others' silence,
them speaking feels like an act of war."*

—

The year was 2020, and unrest was in the ether.

The COVID-19 pandemic began, decimating lives, disrupting economies, and catalyzing those of us who had managed to survive to reevaluate our priorities. It felt as though collectively, humanity was having an existential crisis; as though many of us were asking ourselves "Who am I?" "Why am I here?" "Is this all there is?" Essentially, we were seeking the answer to the question of the ages: "What is my purpose?"

It was no longer enough to plod unconsciously on the treadmill of life. The zeitgeist had shifted.

In the midst of this global shift, Liz and I came into each other's consciousness. Like many of the Black writers and change-makers whom we both now count among our friends, she was extremely active on LinkedIn. By dint of consistently showing up as the embodiment of #BlackExcellence, she started growing a large and engaged community, of which I happily became a part. We connected and started interacting with each other's content.

What began as a mutual admiration fangirling moment has evolved into a friendship. As time passed, Liz and I realized that many of our intersectionalities and interests overlapped.

We are, of course, both Black women of Caribbean extraction. We both have:

- Qualifications on qualifications. (Anybody with Caribbean parents understands this, lol. This is not a brag; it's just facts. Liz having three master's degrees is just business as usual in our culture.)

- Experience with suicidality, depression, domestic violence, and invisible illnesses.

- A similar sense of humor—partly as a coping mechanism. We love to laugh. We love a good meme, a hilarious gif, a pithy turn of phrase, witty banter. Want jokes? We got jokes.

- An appreciation of a statement earring and bold lippie.

- Oceans of innate empathy.

- A strong social justice streak.

- A love of good vibes, cool crystals, and positive affirmations.

- A deep respect and affection for Black folks, especially Black women.

- A desire to speak life into people, and see everyone thrive.

And of course, we both love to write.

In response to the recalibration of the spiritus mundi, Liz wrote about *us*. She posted about Black history, Black culture, Black beauty, and about the challenges of trying to exist in a Black body. I say "trying" because too many of us were unable to live out our days peacefully. So many of us were passing away.

No...that is inaccurate. "Passing away" implies a soft, peaceful slipping into the eternal night. At this juncture in history (like so many others), that is not what was happening to Black people. Our skinfolk were being murdered. Brutally. Daily. With impunity. By the very officials charged to protect and serve us all.

Did Black Lives Matter?

They should. Theoretically they did. But the evidence, captured by cell phones and body cams, said otherwise.

This was another pandemic. Our pandemic. "Ours" because it seemed as if it would fall to us—as usual—to create the cure, administer it, and advocate for changes that would benefit not only us, but also every other marginalized group.

The community mourned. The village mourned. The diaspora mourned.

We mourned Ahmaud Arbery.

We mourned Breonna Taylor.

We mourned George Floyd.

We mourned all of our slain siblings.

And while mourning, while navigating the trauma of seeing people who look like us slain with no penalty or punishment for the perpetrators, Liz sprang fully into action. She found her purpose. She found her voice.

She made a conscious decision to apply her considerable skill as a writer, experience as an educator, and yes, her unapologetic voice, in order to help to make the world a better place. As she explains in the first chapter:

"It wasn't until I witnessed the murder of George Floyd...that I decided I no longer had any desire to censor or suppress my voice, regardless of my past experiences. I needed to be seen. But I also needed to be heard."

Grounded in her newfound calling, Liz ramped up her activity—and her activism. She posted daily, often multiple times a day, teaching, cajoling, admonishing, entertaining, supporting, calling out, calling in. She gathered her community around the virtual break room, held space for her Black and brown siblings, and educated the corporate elite about Black culture, history, trauma, and joy. In my corner of the interwebs, I did the same, as did many of us. Writers, speakers, educators, creators, influencers—we were all determined to use our voices, jointly and severally, to advocate for a more equitable world, in which Black people could be truly free to safely live the life of their choosing.

Liz became one of the de facto leaders of this new movement. She owned her voice, controlled her narrative, and pulled no punches. Her posts were meticulously researched, undergirded by academic rigor, yet also human, compelling, and relatable. Her platform grew exponentially: 80K, 90K, then well over 100,000 followers.

But the beauty of it is that it was never about the followers. It was always about the work. The followers came as a result of Liz showing up boldly, consistently, authentically, and speaking truth to power. Driven by purity of purpose, she evolved into the renowned social justice warrior and content creator we know and love today. She has a voice, and it is a force to be reckoned with.

In the process, Liz inspired thousands of others on LinkedIn (myself included) to be even more fearless and unapologetic in how we showed up on the streets, both on social media and in real life.

Ever the educator, Liz shares knowledge. In *I'm Not Yelling*, she synthesizes the lessons that she has learned from life, corporate America, and social media into a masterclass.

To be clear, the book is not about social media mastery—though that might happen. It is about mastery of your inner self. Mastery of your image. Mastery of your narrative. It takes you on a journey of self-healing, self-discovery, self-advocacy, and self-expression. It provides a roadmap to help you emerge confident, empowered, and living as loudly or quietly as you wish.

The goal is to help you connect with and express the most authentic version of who you are. The goal is to help you stop masking, shrinking, and code switching. The goal is to help you move from existing to living; from merely surviving to joyfully thriving. The goal is to help you reclaim your voice.

"You're on mute" is one of the phrases that has emerged in this post-pandemic era. *I'm Not Yelling* invites us all to un-mute ourselves and let our voices be heard—at whatever volume we choose.

We're not yelling, but we can if we want to.

—**Lisa Hurley**, activist, writer, and speaker

introduction

When I was twelve, I learned a painful lesson—that my voice had the power to kill. I had just read Maya Angelou's *I Know Why the Caged Bird Sings*. Reading about how she stopped talking for five years, until she was thirteen, terrified me. A pivotal moment in Maya's life happened when she was very young. She was sexually assaulted by her mother's boyfriend. After she spoke the name of her attacker, he was killed, the murder presumably committed by one of her uncles. Maya was devastated by what she interpreted to be the destructive power of her own voice. Because she feared what her words might be capable of, she stopped speaking and remained silent for five years.

At twelve, I also began to think long and hard about the potential of my own voice. From reading *I Know Why the Caged Bird Sings* and Maya Angelou's subsequent works, I knew a voice could be transformatively powerful. My hero, Maya Angelou, had gone on to be a trailblazer working for the city of San Francisco as its first Black bus conductor at the age of sixteen. Next, she was a star on stage, touring Europe in a production of *Porgy and Bess*. As a civil rights activist, she worked alongside Malcolm X for Black liberation in Ghana, Africa. She was the very definition of the power she had reclaimed by leaning into everything her voice could be.

Comparatively, my voice didn't seem to stir up much interest at all. It appeared to annoy those around me, if anything. I was extremely interested in what my classmates thought about me. However, my voice tended not to evoke much emotion from them other than amusement, confusion, or resentment. A

Black British child of Jamaican immigrants in South Florida was an anomaly my classmates tolerated but were more inclined to ridicule. As a result, I learned to snap, crack jokes, and cuss; I became the class clown as a matter of survival, rather than for comedic aspirations. I was often the loudest voice in the back of the classroom or at the back of the school bus. In the lunchroom, rather than shrinking from view, I made it my business to be the center of attention. I made sure I targeted my potential attackers before they had the chance to make fun of my English accent, my cheap clothes, and my natural braids that my mother adamantly refused to chemically relax.

Nonetheless, once I got off the bus, I ran home to carefully complete my assignments and study for my upcoming quizzes and tests. My Caribbean immigrant parents were always quick to remind us how much they had sacrificed. It wasn't for us to bring home C's or for the teacher to call them while they were at work to complain that we'd been talking in class. All that studying landed me a full academic scholarship to the top journalism college in my state, where I learned that being loud and outspoken was detrimental to my academic success.

Unlike in my middle and high schools, most of the students and faculty at the University of Florida were white. At my high school of two thousand students, I graduated number five in my class. My loud, outspoken, boisterous persona had been valued and admired. I had been the editor of my school newspaper and an anchor on the morning news show. Our mostly Black teachers encouraged us to speak our minds and empower ourselves by challenging the system. They nurtured our outspokenness and were just as invested in our success as many of our own parents. At the University of Florida, in Gainesville, the philosophy was the total opposite.

On the first day of orientation on campus, we were encouraged by the speaker on stage to look left and look right. We all promptly followed those directions, only to be given a stunning prediction about our future classmates in the large auditorium. He told us that neither of the students sitting on either side of us would make it to graduation. That statement hit me like a punch to the gut. Statistically speaking, we were expected to fail. Leaders at this elite university had already determined it was likely that we wouldn't make it to the graduation stage four years later. The speaker was matter-of-fact and quite nonchalant in delivering this news. There would be no "hand-holding" or encouragement from teachers invested in our success, like I had experienced in high school. By the time I graduated five years later, I'd only had one Black professor—the only professor I'd talked to for more than five minutes the whole time I attended the school.

At the University of Florida, you had to put your nose to the grindstone, work twice as hard as your classmates, and prove that you belonged there. After all, if someone received a job because they were a minority, was it fair that the opportunity was given to them because of the color of their skin? The question was often posed by one of my journalism classmates during class discussions about the merits of these types of "affirmative action" initiatives.

This was the early nineties on the heels of the Rodney King verdict. Top journalism schools around the country were making a huge effort to increase Black representation in newsrooms nationally. This meant recruiting efforts at predominantly Black high schools like mine. Full scholarships, internships, and mentorships were offered to students from historically excluded backgrounds. On several occasions, I remember heated discussions about the fairness of affirmative action and white students in my classes feeling as though it was "unfair." My response was always that affirmative action was attempting to address hundreds of years of policy and practice that had always been unfair. From my own experience as an intern, newsrooms still had very few folks that looked like me. My explanations were typically met with blank stares from my classmates, followed by awkward silences and quick pivots to another topic from professors who also looked nothing like me.

I learned that the loud, boisterous voice I had cultivated so well didn't contribute to my survival in spaces where people didn't look like me. Their curious glances betrayed that they were already wondering how I'd managed to be sitting next to them, questioning whether I truly belonged. Constantly making jokes, as I had in high school, was unseemly considering the gravity of being "allowed" in these spaces. I was the only one who looked like me. I had to represent in a way that showed I took this "privilege" seriously. There was no room for mistakes, because I felt all eyes on me every time I walked into a room.

The most transformative moment of my life was feeling the heavy steel of handcuffs clamped on my wrists. I was placed in the back of a police car when I was just nineteen years old, as a sophomore at the University of Florida. I was falsely accused of shoplifting and arrested. The charges were later dropped, and I won a civil lawsuit against the retail store that had called the police. But in that moment, everything I thought about the world and my place in it changed. For the first time in my life, I felt totally powerless, staring down at my hands and realizing I had no ability to control anything.

For many Black women in corporate America, there is a similar feeling of helplessness and even hopelessness. Perhaps we have other trauma we have had to navigate, and even suppress, just so we can function in predominantly white spaces. We know we are expected to always be perfect, have the answers, and look like we have it all together. Meanwhile, we're slowly falling apart inside.

We feel powerless because we know we can't share any of these feelings for fear of being seen as incompetent. We don't have the ability to empower our voices, so we turn inward, working harder than everyone else. We secretly hope that our work ethic will be rewarded, yet we are always overlooked and undervalued.

Silence became my strategy as I completed my degree and entered the workplace, first in nonprofit organizations, then in media and sales roles, until eventually climbing the ranks of the administrative offices in higher education. I spent more and more time listening rather than speaking. I also learned to moderate my voice in a way that appeared to be appealing in those spaces. I wanted to be accepted, so I tried to present myself in a way that showed I wasn't a threat to the status quo in those environments. I always smiled. I rarely showed my outgoing personality. I was one-note because one-note was safe.

That feeling of safety cultivated by my actions was violated again about a week after May 25, 2020. Everything changed when I inadvertently watched the video of George Floyd being murdered by former police officer Derek Chauvin. I had managed to avoid the video on social media, quickly scrolling whenever I saw the coverage in my feed. But on this day, I was checking work email on my laptop while I sat on the couch. I absently watched the top stories on the cable news channel playing on the flat-screen television on my living room wall. The sound was muted as the headlines flashed across the screen.

Suddenly, without warning, the video of the murder began to flicker on my flat screen. I was totally transfixed. Before I knew it, I was crying uncontrollably, my face contorted in a pain that welled up from the depths of my soul. As I imagined his voice crying out for his mother, I clutched my face and doubled over at the waist. My own son was happily playing with his toys on the floor at my feet. It was at that moment that I knew I had to reclaim my voice. I needed it. It was not negotiable. It was an absolute necessity.

I spent the next week in a mindless fog. I suffered from uncontrollable panic attacks, heart racing and hands shaking at various moments throughout the day. The smallest disruption, such as a broken glass as I loaded the dishwasher, sent me into a tailspin. One day, my children yelled "Put your hands up" while playing cops and robbers. It sent me into a frenzy. I knew I had to do something. I decided that I needed to live in my authentic self. This meant that in every aspect of my life, both at work and at home, I needed to walk in my truth.

That meant I had to shed the pretense that had come to dominate my professional life. Up until that moment, I had been a perfectly curated version of myself. Code-switching—coupled with an insatiable desire to be accepted, curtailing my opinions, and feigning an amiable personality to ensure my acceptance—had become my routine. It was a complement to my perfectly coiffed and chemically processed hair, my conservative dress, my Valley-girl mannerisms, and my total being. Nevertheless, it had put down the mask and displayed the woman I really was. But who was I? I wasn't even sure I knew, and how would I introduce my real self to professional environments?

The process started slowly, first on social media and then on my podcast. I began to express myself in ways I never had before about my angst regarding the direction of the country. I also expressed my own insecurities in professional environments, and my observations of inequities witnessed and experienced over the duration of my career. I grew an engaged following of more than 100,000 people on social media over the course of a year; they supported the evolution and development of my voice. I realized my voice was valid, real, and true. So many Black women not only related to my experiences but also shared their own. My mission has evolved into showing other Black women how to achieve this freedom. It comes from embracing this mantra of authenticity, which has brought me such a keen sense of emotional well-being and peace of mind.

This book is a treasure trove of all the things I learned from researching the experiences of Black women in professional spaces and a road map to freedom. It's a clarion call to embrace our true authentic selves. It's also a community narrative of everything I experienced, as well as the stories I heard from the Black women who followed me. These women shared instances of not being hired for jobs they were more than qualified for; they talked about the microaggressions they endured when they were hired; they recounted tales of being passed over for positions and not being promoted despite their diligent work and credentials. These women second-guessed their very existences.

I was relieved to realize I wasn't alone. But I was also desperate to find answers to their questions. Where did we get the idea that we couldn't show up at work as our real selves? Why did we feel we couldn't speak authentically, dress in ways that highlight our personal styles and express our personalities, while keeping it classy, or even wear our hair naturally as it grew out of our heads? Who told us the selves we presented in every other environment were not professional or acceptable once we stepped into our workplaces? And why were we the only ones so uncomfortable in our own skins, while everyone else seemed so at ease? Why were so many of us experiencing imposter syndrome, and what did that even mean?

I made it my mission to find out, to provide to my community the answers backed up by research, and to share strategies to overcome the challenges we were all experiencing. And I want to share those findings with you throughout the chapters of this book, so you can take advantage of the lessons I was able to learn over the course of the year that I spent engaging with thousands of Black women on social media.

I learned so many lessons in these interactions with women in media, marketing, government, nonprofit, community advocacy, education, business, healthcare, diversity, equity and inclusion, technology, and small business about the ability to exude confidence, to command promotions or a higher salary, to articulate your value in corporate and business spaces, to take advantage of any and all opportunities that present themselves to you, and to leverage your voice to amplify your brand.

This book will help you to understand that it's not your lack of work ethic that's holding you back, but the lack of experience in acknowledging the strength of your own personal story. You will also learn how to articulate that story to develop your own personal brand narrative that can be used in corporate spaces or for business opportunities outside the workplace. Or perhaps you will decide to do a combination of both.

You will learn the difference between imposter syndrome and the valid reaction to trauma from having microaggressions perpetrated on you because of your natural hair, mannerisms, dress code, and qualifications. By identifying strategies to address these toxic behaviors, you can confront them head-on. You can avoid behaviors contributing to your trauma, such as code-switching and assimilation, and determine whether those places really deserve your presence.

If those spaces are not conducive to honoring your true self, you will be able to articulate your value and pursue opportunities elsewhere by leveraging the tools you learn about developing networks of like-minded Black women or others who serve as mentors and sponsors and constitute a support network.

I am a twenty-year veteran of higher education who has worked in nonprofit, media, and sales. I spent more than a decade as a college professor and a director in the corporate office of my institution before using my voice to create a platform of influence on LinkedIn. I grew a following of more than 100,000 people in less than a year and, by doing so, I garnered national attention and was interviewed by the *New York Times*, *Forbes*, and *Time* magazine. I also had the opportunity to write for CNN and NBC and was offered the opportunity to start a podcast on the Ebony Covering Black America Podcast Network. Most recently, I entered into partnerships and sponsorships with major brands like Dove (to promote the passage of the federal CROWN Act) and Forever 21 (to promote their Black History Month clothing collection featuring Black designers).

Every single one of these opportunities came because I harnessed the power of my real voice. This meant amplifying and articulating my worth, and stepping into each possibility with confidence, knowing that I added value to all of them.

Are you ready to learn how to find your voice? Keep reading.

chapter 1

how it began

"You can't know where you're going
unless you know where you came from."

—Maya Angelou

Who are you? No, really. Who are you? Have you thought about who you are, how you feel, and how you act when you are at your most comfortable and feeling like your most authentic self? What does that look like to you?

When I decided I wanted to live my truth in every way, I struggled through an identity crisis because I realized I honestly didn't know who I was. I had been code-switching for so long, imitating what I thought was acceptable based on the norms I had encountered in predominantly white spaces. I didn't even know what my true voice and personality was like in its entirety, full and rich. It had always been moderated to some extent, even at home with my husband and kids! Most of my waking hours were spent at work with my organization leaders, coworkers, and clients, so I spent the least amount of time around friends and family.

But I even found myself affecting my work persona at home, as necessary. My husband would be on the phone with a bill collector and ask me to have "Angela" talk to them. Angela is my middle name, and it's what my husband called the voice I used to code-switch with bill collectors. I'd let them know they would receive our payment by the end of the week. I might even use it to talk to the manager at the store to complain about poor service. The voice sounded like an irritated Valley girl—higher-pitched than my own, naturally deeper voice. Angela's words were more hurried and clipped than my own. Mine is more of a low, slow Southern drawl. But whenever I used Angela's voice, I would get my point across quickly. Of course, a payment extension was usually forthcoming as well! The manager had better quickly resolve any issues I had, because that voice indicated to everyone in earshot that I meant business.

The version of "Angela" I used at work was a lot more easy-going. I was likable. I was safe. I didn't rock the boat. Angela agreed with most proposed initiatives, even if she didn't necessarily think they were sound ideas. She was the coworker who would play along to get along because she didn't want to be labeled as an

"Angry Black Woman." It was imperative not to speak up too loudly about her own opinions, gently offering suggestions and backing off quickly if they didn't appear to be well received. She listened intently and nodded congenially when appropriate. She didn't even object when supervisors or coworkers stole her ideas and presented them in meetings as their own. "Hey! Teamwork makes the dream work! Right, Angela?" High-five!

I made sure that my appearance assimilated to all the environments I worked in; first in nonprofit agencies, media, and sales roles, then later in higher education. In each environment, I learned that blending into my surroundings was safest. So, Angela came out again. That translated to my perfectly pressed hair and muted makeup; my business-professional, conservative, monotone dress code; and my mannerisms too. Morning routines were hours long, using gold-plated curling irons in multiple barrel sizes to press my relaxed hair as straight as possible and laid to the gods. Makeup needed to be glamorous enough to show I cared about my appearance but not so glam that I stood out significantly from my peers. The goal was to be sure clothing was perceived as professional and blended in. Skirts and pantsuits were always black or navy blue. They were just a little more conservatively styled than my coworkers', just to be absolutely on the safe side.

But where did I get the idea that I needed to be an alternative version of myself? I scoured my memory to try to figure it out. Where exactly did it come from?

I was born in the UK to Jamaican parents. My parents had both immigrated to London and met as teenagers. They had been taught the value of diligent work by their own parents, who were immigrants as well. My mother was a nurse who had started nursing school at the age of seventeen, right out of secondary school. My father was a mechanic who had worked for London Transport on Britain's iconic red buses for as long as I could remember. They both believed in doing whatever you had to do to be successful, even if that meant moving halfway across the world. I was almost twelve when they made the difficult decision to move the entire family to America—the land of opportunity. We landed in South Florida, where I was served complete culture shock with a side of fear and confusion.

I had attended a primary school in the heart of London, where I was one of only three Black children in my class. We moved to a predominantly Black neighborhood in the heart of South Florida. The only white people at the school I attended were teachers, and even they were few and far between. I knew that a huge part of understanding the American Black experience in my adopted home was learning about Black culture and embracing this knowledge with every fiber of my being.

My mother had always encouraged my love of reading. Some of my first books were by Jane Austen—*Pride and Prejudice, Emma,* and *Sense and Sensibility*. But once we moved to America, I realized I had little in common with Elizabeth Bennet and her sisters. I needed to broaden the scope of my reading list quick, fast, and in a hurry.

I dove into reading the works of Richard Wright, Donald Goines, Alice Walker, Maya Angelou, Zora Neale Hurston, and Toni Morrison. Understanding Black folk was critical because that's what I saw in the mirror, reflected in my surroundings every day. I devoured book after book. There was no internet back then, so a bus ride to the library became a weekly pilgrimage. It culminated with an obsessive exploration of the card catalog, searching for hidden treasure. This knowledge was essential to my survival, as I absorbed the musings of Alex Haley, Dr. Frances Cress Welsing, and Carter G. Woodson. They all told me secrets my parents didn't know.

I'd watched them struggle to support my younger brothers and me. We all lived in one bedroom at my grandmother's house. She had immigrated to Florida a few years before us. My parents immediately returned to school to pick up where they left off in the occupations they had in London. They both worked full-time jobs while they attended school, Mom as a nursing assistant in a nursing home, Dad as a groundskeeper for the City of Fort Lauderdale during the day and a 7-Eleven cashier in the evenings. They showed me that failure was not an option and that there was no sacrifice too great to be able to succeed and aspire to your professional and career goals.

I wasn't aware of the statistics at the time, but I would be overcoming virtually insurmountable odds to even graduate and attend college. According to the Education Trust,[1] while Black students attend schools that are underfunded, they also have less access to experienced teachers, a full range of math and science courses, school counselors, and gifted/talented, advanced placement, and international baccalaureate programs. Black students get the illusion of education without the critical components of a quality education. This systemic approach to denying Black students a quality education has resulted in inequities in high school graduation, college enrollment, graduation rates, and degree attainment.

My parents weren't aware of these grim statistics either. As far as they knew, America was the land of opportunity regardless of where you attended school. My job was to report to school, work hard, and bring home the highest grades possible. After all, it was the least I could do, considering all the sacrifices my parents had made to bring me to the land of opportunity! Despite the merciless bullying I endured daily, I tried my best and forged ahead in seventh grade. I knew my parents would accept nothing less. My upbringing in South Florida

---

1   Jr, Marshall Anthony, Andrew Howard Nichols, and Wil Del Pilar. "Raising Undergraduate Degree Attainment among Black Women and Men Takes on New Urgency amid the Pandemic." *The Education Trust*, May 13, 2021. edtrust.org/resource/national-and-state-degree-attainment-for-black-women-and-men.

primed me to be as bold, confident, and outspoken as I possibly could be. Being meek and quiet meant being picked on, so I became loud and unapologetic.

Growing up in a predominantly Black neighborhood in the heart of Fort Lauderdale, I was less than twenty minutes from Miami. I saw that the most popular kids in my middle school were bold in every move they made. The girls on the school bus, in my classes, and in the lunchroom were audacious and loud. They wore fluorescent spandex, bright-colored makeup, multi-colored braids, and bamboo earrings. Their bangles jingled loudly as they animatedly moved their arms when they spoke. Each point and syllable was emphasized with a clap of their hands, a kiss of the teeth, or a loud smack of the mouth—one that would be even louder if they were chewing gum. I was mesmerized by those girls and vowed to be just like them—the type of girl who said whatever was on her mind and didn't back down, no matter what.

In high school, I became the editor of the school's newspaper and an anchor on our news station. Speaking up at every chance became a daily routine, and I never moderated or dialed down my voice or tone. My accent was now the adopted drawl of my South Florida peers, with loose speech punctuated by shoulder shrugs and exaggerated raised eyebrows and lips poked out as needed. My school was over 90 percent Black, with most of my classmates coming from what would be considered low-income households. Most of us qualified for free lunch because we were below the poverty line, even though we didn't use it because school lunch was "nasty." Instead, we would break the school rules by leaving campus during lunch. We gathered enough change to buy pickled hot sausages or beef patties at the convenience store on the corner. Then we stood outside the chain-link fence and savored their deliciousness until the bell rang.

The chain-link fence offered scant separation from the dilapidated houses surrounding the school. Guys from the neighborhood, with heavy gold rope chains around their necks and matching gold grills decorating their cocky smiles, hung out on the corners outside. They flashed wads of cash, designer clothes, and sneakers most of us thought we would never be able to afford. Some of them rode around in box Chevy cars with rag tops, sporting Gucci or Louis Vuitton logos woven into the vinyl. The candy paint jobs glistened in the hot South Florida sun just like the chrome twenty-four-inch rims. Despite the contradictions we witnessed around us, our teachers, who were mostly Black, encouraged us to focus on success, graduation, and life beyond the east side of Fort Lauderdale. They wore kente cloth, brown wooden beads, and black medallions. They stressed that we were the descendants of African Kings and Queens. My junior year, my American government teacher, a Black man who was active in city government, recommended I read Cheikh Anta Diop's *The African Origin of Civilization*. It was in that moment that I embraced the idea that my identity was one of greatness and royalty in the embodiment of Blackness.

Emmanuel Kulu, who I interviewed for the *Black Power Moves* podcast, is the author of *I, Pharaoh*. He explains[2] why this type of knowledge is essential in the development of young Black minds. "My parents brought me up...knowing my history—my father being from Cameroon from the Zulu tribe and my mother being from the heart of the Civil Rights Movement right here in Chicago. My mother was affiliated with the Black Panther Movement, so when they met, I had the Black American side, and then I had my African side. [...] I was always enlightened on these great ancient African kingdoms, including Egypt. One day, when we had a project to describe a great person of antiquities...of ancient history, my father and I made this beautiful project by painting his face brown. It was about King Tut, and the teacher gave me a B minus. I watched my father argue with my teacher because the teacher said it was historically inaccurate. The only reason why is because he was a Black man. So, since the third grade, that lit a fire into me."

---

2   Kulu, Emmanuel. "Restoring the True African Imagery of Ancient Egypt." Interview by Elizabeth Leiba. *Black Power Moves, EBONY Covering Black America Podcast Network*, April 15, 2022. ebonypodcastnetwork.com/black-power-moves.

The African historian continues, "My father used to tell me the saying, 'What you do for yourself depends on what you think of yourself. What you think of yourself depends on what you know of yourself. What you know of yourself depends on what you've been told.' So, it's time to change the narrative of what we've been told."

Dr. Nadia Lopez explains why it is so significant for Black children to be taught by teachers who look like them and to be inspired by teachers invested in their success. She decided to give students more opportunities to study the sciences, technology, engineering, arts, and math. She is the award-winning educator who became a viral sensation after the popular blog *Humans of New York* featured her as one of the most influential people. Dr. Lopez founded Mott Hall Bridges Academy, a STEAM-focused middle school in Brownsville, Brooklyn, New York, in 2010, and served as the principal for ten years. She was named among LinkedIn's 2019 Top 10 Voices in Education and received the Black Girls Rock award, alongside Michelle Obama, in 2015.

"We teach our children the boring way so that, this way, they only go into entry-level positions, but they don't think about becoming producers," Dr. Lopez emphasizes.[3] "I wanted to remix what education looked like. I wanted to bring them opportunities to meet people who look like them who were doing things. Let them learn about the astrophysicists. [...] We could teach them about building rockets, [but] I'm not excited about the Mentos and the Coca Cola and seeing it explode. I want them to actually meet astrophysicists and talk about their journey to getting into that position and then what opportunities come with that robust experience."

She continues, "You see that, children who have great potential but don't have the resources, [they] have never left the immediate community, dealing with all types of abuses and temporary housing. There was just such a divide between

---

3   Leiba, Elizabeth, and Nadia Lopez. "Unaired Episode." Produced by the Ebony Podcast
     Network. *Black Power Moves.*

children because they were being told that they weren't going to go anywhere, that they weren't going to get to college. And that broke my heart because they just needed someone to understand and listen to them. No one was taking that time because they were so focused on getting through the instruction. So, I created a space that allowed children to know that they were exceptional."

Teachers like Dr. Lopez shaped my formative years in learning that I was exceptional. High school graduation came all too soon, and my arrival on the college campus in North Florida was a major culture shock. I realized that I was now a small fish in a humongous pond, and blending in without making anyone feel uncomfortable was most advantageous. Rather than wanting to be seen, I wanted to disappear, hoping to skate by, pass my classes, and not disappoint my parents. Unlike my high school teachers, the majority of whom had looked like me and encouraged us to be bold and confident, my college professors didn't even seem to see me. Their eyes didn't register recognition when they spoke to me, as if they were looking right through me. Most made it clear they didn't care about our academic success. If we didn't pass, they told us it was probably because we didn't belong there to begin with. They explained it was for the best, to weed out the weakest amongst us.

At orientation, we were advised to look both left and right because neither of those individuals would be there at graduation. I took note and made sure that I looked and acted like I belonged because I wanted to be sure I remained the student in the middle; I wanted to be the one striding across the stage to grab my diploma while my parents clapped proudly in the audience. Because of the pressure, I became meek and unsure of myself. Rather than excelling, I was a middle-of-the-road student, holding on for dear life to maintain the GPA needed to maintain scholarship eligibility. It was a world of difference from high school, where I had graduated fifth in a class of two hundred. The University of Florida had a student body of more than fifty thousand. I felt lost and alone. Most of my classmates looked nothing like me. Neither did my professors. The safest bet was not to attract additional attention from their disengaged eyes. They'd already made it clear my success was not their concern, so I internalized that idea and acted accordingly. I couldn't afford to draw their ire. Failing classes was not an option for a student attending on scholarship. Unlike in South Florida, I found that my boisterous, exaggerated confidence and loud and vivacious ways were not an advantage on the campus in Gainesville, the country town in North Florida.

The long-term success of my strategy to be quiet and assimilate, so I could be accepted and successful in this strange environment, was finally challenged on a Sunday during my sophomore year. My morning had begun quite typically. I'd slipped out of bed in my dorm, grabbed a hoodie, pulled some baggy shorts over my hips, and slung my JanSport bookbag over my shoulder. I headed off campus, leaving my roommate sleeping soundly. I needed to drop some film off at Eckerd's Pharmacy. As the historian for a volunteer organization on campus, it was my job to document our activities, which included feeding the homeless and playing bingo with elderly patients at the local nursing home.

I hoped to drop the film off quickly so I could get back to campus and get some studying done. I was pretty sure I also needed to do some laundry before my week started. Therefore, it was minutes before I was headed right back out the double doors and through the black plastic theft detection mechanism on my way out of the store. It lit up red and beeped so loudly that I physically jumped and spun around to see if the cashier by the register at the door could help.

"Did you buy anything?" he inquired.

I shook my head no, as I headed to his register and plopped my bookbag on the counter.

"I just dropped some film off," I explained hastily.

"Do you mind if I take a look in your bag?" he asked quizzically. "Maybe something set the alarm off."

I shrugged. "Well, I didn't buy anything," I insisted. "But that's fine."

I was anxious to get on with my day, and if this was what he needed to do to be Employee of the Month, I was happy to oblige. I unzipped the bag and opened it with a flourish, wanting to be done with this process as quickly as possible. I rifled a few folders to the side, hoping to satisfy his curiosity. But his eyes had flashed in recognition at something he saw.

"What's that?" he asked.

I looked down. "Oh! I bought that for my camera when I was in here a couple of days ago," I explained. I hadn't even remembered it was in there—a sealed pack of four AA batteries.

"Do you have the receipt?" he asked.

I paused for a second. I knew I had the receipt. It was my habit to save all my receipts. My mother had taught me that custom at a young age because you never knew when you might need to return an item or produce proof that you had purchased it. Considering that the cost of this item, no matter how small, could be submitted to my organization for reimbursement, I knew I had to have kept it. Now, to find it. I began to rifle frantically through the bag.

This conversation was starting to take a turn that I didn't like. And the cashier was progressing from a minor annoyance in my day to someone who looked like he was about to cause a major problem. He was already on a small phone next to his station explaining the situation to someone, though I wasn't sure whom. Whomever it was would be able to resolve this, I felt sure. I felt better and paused in my rummaging to wait for the manager.

A slim, pale-skinned woman with an expressionless face and straight brown hair pulled back in a bun appeared at his side. He quickly explained the situation to her, while I waited for her to take the offending security tag off, put on a sticker that said "Paid" on the package, or do whatever she needed to do. I needed to be on my way about the real business of my day. But she didn't. Instead, she asked if I would accompany her to her office. Within minutes, I was in a small office in the back of the store with my bookbag on my lap.

"Well, since you can't produce the receipt for the item, we're going to have to have you sign this," she explained matter-of-factly, as she sat down in her chair across from me.

My hands were shaking as I reached for the stark, white sheet she had slid across the brown desk. The words seemed to blur together. I started to panic, as I realized we weren't in her office to resolve this misunderstanding.

"What is this?" I stuttered.

"It's called a 'No Trespass Warning,'" she explained, again with no emotion in her voice. "It means that you are admitting to shoplifting the batteries and based on that fact, you agree to never enter this store again. If you are found in violation of that warning, we can call the police."

I was confused. "I'm not signing that," I said slowly and deliberately. "I told you I bought the batteries a couple of days ago. I'm not signing something that says I stole them because...I didn't."

"So, where's the receipt?" she retorted quickly.

I rifled through my bookbag again, my hands shaking. "I don't know. I mean, I know I have it," I stammered. "It must be here somewhere. But I'm not signing that," I said disgustedly gesturing toward the offensive sheet that I had politely placed right back down on her desk. She could put it back in her filing cabinet or wherever she got it from.

I folded my arms across my chest, trying to calm myself down. My heart was racing, but I knew I couldn't lose my composure. I tried to reason with her. I had been thinking about law school after journalism school. This was my opportunity to use logic on this woman, who so clearly didn't understand I had absolutely no reason to steal.

I explained that I was a sophomore at UF. I was a good student. I came in there all the time to shop. I had walked right into the store and right out without stopping or even stepping anywhere near the batteries. Couldn't she check the security cameras, where she was bound to be able to confirm the truth of my story for herself?

She listened quietly. Her face remained expressionless, as she explained that if I refused to sign the warning, she would call the police. From there she would have me arrested for shoplifting, letting them know I had stolen the batteries in my possession.

"I'm not signing that," I said firmly again.

She picked up the phone and within minutes, an officer from Gainesville Police Department was inside her office, standing next to me. He asked the same questions. Had I bought the batteries? Yes. Where was the receipt? I had looked for it in my bookbag but wasn't able to find it. Would I sign the No Trespass Warning? No. Why not? Because I hadn't stolen the batteries. He informed me that, that being the case, I was giving him no option but to take me to jail. Resigned to my fate on what was now Sunday afternoon, I followed him outside to the parking lot behind the store. There, he handcuffed me and placed me in the back of his police car.

I sat there in a daze as he appeared to be filling out paperwork on the events that had occurred. Another officer pulled up and they chatted casually. It didn't feel real, almost like an out-of-body experience. I looked down at my wrists in the handcuffs. There were no handles on the inside of the doors. The windows were tinted. I could see out, but no one would be able to see me inside. We drove to the outskirts of the city to the jail.

When I was being processed, the officers at the jail thought I was brought to the wrong facility. Despite my baby face and weighing barely 110 pounds, I was nineteen years old. I did belong there and not in the juvenile jail down the street, the officer who had arrested me reassured them. I was fingerprinted, searched, and my mug shot was taken. But because they still didn't feel comfortable placing me in a jail cell with the rest of the inmates, the corrections officers let me sit in the larger holding area, where I was mostly alone. They knew I wouldn't be there overnight since I planned to post bond, so it seemed unnecessary to issue me jail clothes, bedding, and flip-flops that I wouldn't need. However, they had stripped me of all my personal effects, including my bookbag.

The customary one phone call was used to call my mother. A trauma nurse who was used to stressful situations, Mom appeared calm on the phone when I explained what had happened. I told her I would need her to pay my seven-hundred-dollar bond immediately in Fort Lauderdale because it would take a few hours to post in the system and get me released. In the meantime, she would need to drive the five hours to pick me up, since I didn't know anyone with a car who would be able to drive the five miles from campus to pick me up from the jail. She wrote down all the directions, knew exactly what needed to be done, and calmly reassured me she would see me in a few hours. Later, she would confide that she had collapsed into a crying, inconsolable heap on the floor as soon as she hung up the phone with me.

Eventually, my bond registered in the system, hours later. I was processed out and my personal items, including my bookbag, were returned. I sat in the waiting room until my mother arrived. I leapt into the passenger side next to her, happy to be free of that place, feeling dirty, defeated, cold, and tired. My mother was relieved but confused. She asked me rapid-fire questions that I tried to answer as best I could. One question I couldn't answer was why I hadn't just signed the No Trespass Warning. Why hadn't I signed it? If I had, they would have just let me go. I would have been at the dorm resting, maybe watching TV with my roommate, or studying as I had resolved to do that morning. Instead, I was here, processing the events of the worst day of my young life.

I didn't have a simple answer. All I knew was that I couldn't sign that piece of paper. I knew I hadn't stolen, so how could I sign something saying I had? It went against everything my parents had taught me. I was only half-surprised at my mother's confusion as to why I had taken such a stern stand. In her mind, the easiest course of action, with the least amount of friction and inconvenience, would have been the most suitable. After all, she was an immigrant. She knew what it meant to swallow her pride and do things that seemed unfair, like go back to school for a job she had been performing in another country since she was a teenager. It seemed incredible to her that I had been so defiant in that moment when it wasn't necessary.

I tried to explain to her that it was necessary to me. I took that stand because, at that moment, I knew what was happening wasn't fair. I had spent the first two years of college adapting, adjusting, and changing the way I acted, talked, and appeared to adhere to the rules in spaces where I wasn't expected to belong. The faculty at UF had made it clear that they were under no obligation to help me succeed, especially when I probably wouldn't be there for long. Despite my isolation, I'd worked as hard as I could to be successful; I had done everything I was supposed to do, down to keeping the receipt for an item that cost $2.49, just like she taught me. But none of those precautions had prevented me from being accused of something I hadn't done, and I'd simply refused to go along with the lie. Wasn't it enough that, to survive on campus, I'd had to create a quiet, reserved persona at the expense of the empowered Black girl I had grown to be? I'd sacrificed my own essence. Enough was enough. I had to draw the line somewhere, and this was it.

I was frustrated by the fact that my mother didn't appear to understand my rationale. I grabbed the backpack and started rifling through it again. At that moment, I spotted a bright red folder in the back of my bag and began flipping through the notepad sheets inside. Finally, I slipped my fingers into the side pocket of the folder, and between them slid the receipt I had been looking for all day. I started crying hysterically.

The next day, my mother retained an attorney. As soon as he saw the receipt, he filed a motion to have the charges of petty theft dropped by the state attorney's office. Of course, it happened immediately once he sent them a copy of the receipt. The four-pack of AA batteries had cost $2.49. The question of whether I should have my arrest record sealed and expunged came up. Because the charge was a minor one and had been dropped, my attorney recommended not sealing my records. His rationale was that any government agency that really wanted to know if I had ever been arrested would be able to find out that information if they did an extensive enough background check. Besides, because the charges were dropped, there was a presumption that I had been innocent of any wrongdoing. His fear was also that, since Florida law only allows for one opportunity to expunge a criminal record, that meant that if anything more serious were to happen in the future, I would have already used my only chance; he didn't want me to lose that insurance policy of being able to expunge my record if I had any other similar interactions with police in the future. Later, I would be grateful that he gave me that advice after additional negative encounters with the police in my adulthood. I was glad to have that insurance!

Later, as I became a professional, I worked in spaces like higher education that required background checks. I invariably felt trepidation whenever it was confirmed by human resources that I would need to complete a background check. Were they judging me when they saw I had an arrest on my record? Did they think there might be some validity to the charge, even though it had been dropped? An accusation still felt shameful to me. Did they think I was a thief? Later, all those questions would go through my mind and create a great deal of shame around this incident, making me want to bury the memory of everything that had happened.

Once my attorney successfully filed for the charges to be dropped, he advised me to pursue a lawsuit against Eckerd's for calling the police and having me arrested. He explained it was at their discretion whether to notify the police regarding the situation or not. And he also confided that, as a middle-aged white man, he had been practicing law in the city of Gainesville for more than a decade and had never seen the police called for anyone stealing an item that cost a couple of bucks. He was quite surprised and said the only explanation he could see was a case of racial profiling. Based on that fact and the stand I had taken by not signing the No Trespass Warning, he asked if I wanted to pursue civil action. He cautioned that I wouldn't get rich or score a huge amount in compensatory damages from the company. But what it would do was to send a clear message to Eckerd's that their behavior had been unacceptable. I agreed! It would take another three years to win a lawsuit against the company for false arrest and malicious prosecution. I walked away with $10,000. After paying the attorney's fees, I ended up with about seven thousand dollars. But for me it felt like a million-dollar judgment. I finally felt vindicated. The jury had listened to my case, and they agreed with me. What Eckerd's had done to me was wrong.

Since it took several years for the civil suit to be resolved, I had quite some time to process the implications of my arrest. I was about to enter the workforce after graduation. People wouldn't know me or my honest intentions. No one would know that the real reason I was arrested was because I refused to admit to doing something I hadn't done. They wouldn't be aware that the item I had been accused of stealing only cost $2.49. They would simply see an arrest appear on the background check. I thought about the words of my lawyer, however, and decided against sealing my records. If this could happen once, was there any guarantee it might not happen again? I had already experienced a complete loss of innocence and the destruction of my trust in law enforcement. Whenever I spotted a police car in my rearview mirror, or saw one pull up alongside me in traffic, my heart immediately started racing. My body became tense, and my hands gripped the wheel more tightly. I was now afraid of the police.

I didn't know it at the time, but as a victim of racial profiling, my situation as a Black teenager had been far from unique. And as I entered adulthood, I would become familiar with the names of other Black women, like Atatiana Jefferson, Rekia Boyd, Sandra Bland, and Breonna Taylor, who had also been racially profiled like I was but had far more tragic circumstances as a result of being arrested. But even though I had yet to learn those names, I had a loss of innocence in knowing that this could happen to me. I could be targeted based on what someone in a position of power thought about me. And their perception would be largely framed by the color of my skin. It was a sobering reality check.

According to the nonprofit organization Prison Policy Initiative,[4] Black women are more likely than white or Latina women to be stopped by police. And 2015 survey data shows that Black women were at least as likely as white men to be detained during a stop; white women, meanwhile, were about half as likely as white men to be arrested during a stop. Black women were arrested in 4.4 percent of police-initiated stops, which was roughly three times as often as white women (1.5 percent), and twice as often as Latinas (2.2 percent). In addition, during a police-initiated stop, use of force rates were higher for Black women than white or Latina women.

---

4   Prison Policy Initiative. "Policing Women: Race and Gender Disparities in Police Stops, Searches, and Use of Force." Prison Policy Initiative, 2019. www.prisonpolicy.org/blog/2019/05/14/policingwomen.

Prince George's County, Maryland's state attorney Aisha Braveboy provides some additional insights[5] based on her own experience, from both a background in psychology and her knowledge of restorative justice programs. "I said to myself, 'I will never work for the state's attorney's office. I don't want to lock up Black men!' I mean, that was my belief back then, in the late 1990s. And, as you can imagine, back then we're still talking about this disparate sentencing for crack cocaine and powder cocaine and mass incarceration of young Black men [and] young brown men and women."

She explains further: "That's around the time I started seeing more young women and girls getting into the criminal justice system, and I was like, 'There's no way I would ever be [a part of that].' But seriously, what I thought then and what I know now [are] two very different things. I recognized that a lot of these young people just needed some structure. They needed someone to believe in them, and oftentimes they needed support for their families. [...] So, the question is: how [does] the system of justice ensure...that those people don't return? What else can we do in other ways, especially for us to treat people who commit lower-level offenses? And is incarceration the only answer?"

My arrest and subsequent fight to clear my name, despite my eventual vindication in winning the lawsuit, made me retreat even further into my shell. Despite doing everything the right way, excelling in high school, going on to college on a full scholarship, and attempting to blend into my environment, I had still been arrested. Being my bold and audacious high school self was not an option. I shrank from any opportunities to be the center of attention. In fact, I wanted to be as far away from being noticed as possible. I ended up abandoning my goal of becoming a newspaper reporter. The trauma from my arrest left the remainder of my sophomore year, and subsequently my grades, in shambles. I sleepwalked through my last two years, doing the bare minimum to get through my program.

---

5   Braveboy, Aisha. "Compassionate Criminal Justice Reform." Interview by Elizabeth Leiba. *Black Power Moves, EBONY Covering Black America Podcast Network*, March 24, 2022. ebonypodcastnetwork.com/black-power-moves.

I just wanted to get as far away from the campus as possible. I wanted to forget what had happened there, and I wanted to forget the pain I felt as a result.

The trauma I experienced remained largely unpacked. I saw it as something that was best left unaddressed and forgotten. I made a halfhearted attempt to speak with a mental health counselor for students on campus. But she seemed unable to relate to the anxiety I now felt almost constantly. Her brow furrowed as she wrote furiously on her notepad and tried to understand why the memory of the incident was causing me so much pain. I chose another alternative, which was to try to forget the incident ever happened.

Ashley McGirt, MSW, LCSW, a racial trauma therapist and founder of WA/ CA Therapy Fund Foundation, explains[6] how racial trauma compounds the challenges of seeking mental health therapy for Black people, especially due to the dearth of Black mental health providers:

"Well, your story is my story. It is the story of so many other Black women, so many other Black people who look like us and are presented with these challenges. When I was young, my grandmother passed away, and I experienced grief that turned into major depression. I ended up seeing a counselor who was a white woman, and she did not understand the role of grandmother[s] in Black families. She didn't understand anything about Black culture. Here I was, educating this white woman on Black life; on the intricacies of race, relationships, at nine years old."

"I actually wanted to be a lawyer," she continues. "I was really obsessed with the law, and I just knew that was the path that I wanted to take. But through the experience of losing my grandmother and having these sessions with this white woman who didn't understand me, I told my mom what was going on. She

---

6   McGirt, Ashley. "Black Mental Health Matters." Interview by Elizabeth Leiba. *Black Power Moves, EBONY Covering Black America Podcast Network*, January 18, 2022. ebonypodcastnetwork.com/black-power-moves.

searched and searched and tried to find a Black therapist for me, and she didn't. [...] I experienced a huge bout of depression. I'm like, 'There's got to be other Black children, other Black people, who are experiencing these things. And we should not have to spend our therapy session educating the counselor on what life is like for Black people in America.' So, I did a whole 360°."

She concludes, "I still love the law. I still do a lot of work... [related to] criminal justice [and] ending mass incarceration, but ultimately, I wanted to understand depression, suicidal ideation. My research is on African American suicide because I suffered from those things. I didn't want to live when my grandmother passed away. I didn't understand death. [...] I do a lot of work around death and dying. I also ended up being a hospice therapist, and the majority of my Black hospital patients were extremely young, like my grandmother, who died at sixty-two years old. My grandmother passed [away] from a stroke. The leading cause of stroke is stress. What is it about the Black community that we are so stressed? Well, racism, systemic oppression, all these different things, and I'm a social justice advocate at my core."

Dr. Wizdom Powell, PhD, chief social impact and diversity officer at Headspace and clinical psychologist, observes[7] that there is also a lack of accessible skills, strategies, and tools to navigate the trauma we inhabit daily:

"I think that we have not really honored the tried-and-true traditions of becoming well in Black communities. We have been healing radically for four-hundred-plus years, since 1619, and we are still *here*...not just existing...we're thriving in some ways, even with all the onslaught of racialized violence and degradation. We still are moving and shaking and contributing to [the] world. Imagine a world without us in it. Like, I can't. [...] We are doing so much daily to heal, grow, and thrive,

---

7   Powell, PhD, Wizdom. "Healing Trauma to Improve Emotional Well-Being in Black Communities." Interview by Elizabeth Leiba. *Black Power Moves, EBONY Covering Black America Podcast Network*, January 10, 2020. ebonypodcastnetwork.com/black-power-moves.

and I think the first thing we have to do is honor those traditions, air them out, share [them] with the world, because people don't get how is it that we're still here and still active and engaged and smiling at each other. How are we doing that? There's wisdom that we need to share with the world."

She adds, "The first narrative change—this idea that Black folk don't want to get well or that we don't want to pay attention to our mental and emotional wellness—doesn't really square up with all the healing work we've been doing over time. [...] Secondly, we have to start having different conversations in our community about what constitutes strength. This idea that we're supposed to leap over structural disadvantage, racialized violence, [and] systematic oppression in a single bound...it's mythic—like superheroes are. We need to really start telling ourselves the truth about who we are. And what we are here to do is to experience a range of emotions, from anger to sadness to shame [to] disappointment. All of those are valid, and we have to honor that and hold space for those emotional experiences. Third, we need to be helping each other find the pathways to those supports earlier on, so I'm really, really passionate about youth mental health because if we don't fight for them, then our children, their children, and their children's children will have to do the work that we avoided."

"Times have changed," she continues. "But we have to still honor those traditions, and more importantly we have to make it okay for us to have those issues. Stop telling people that they should push through adversity. Or when someone asks you, 'How are you doing, queen?' You go, 'Well, you know how I'm doing. I'm making it.' Tell the truth and shame the devil! Tell folks how you're really doing, so folks can show up for you in the ways that we should show up for one another. [...] And more important, as a field, this is me speaking to the people who make decisions and write checks: We need to be reconstituting community mental health services for Black and Brown communities because we're not going to show up in those traditional spaces so that people have access to a range of tools and resources that meet them where they are."

Because I was unable to find anyone who looked like me to unpack the trauma, very few people knew about the incident. I wanted to bury every minute of it after I graduated. I entered education because it was a safe career, not competitive and "cut-throat" like journalism. But when I entered education, every school I worked for would run a background check as a formality. My arrest record would show up each time for HR to peruse. Because the charges had been dropped, I knew it wouldn't automatically disqualify me. However, I also knew that a charge of theft couldn't be looked at favorably by anyone who saw it. I tried to overcompensate by being the perfect employee. I felt a deep sense of shame, despite no wrongdoing.

In response to the judgment that was surely happening, I tried to shape myself into someone who wouldn't arouse any suspicion or attract too much attention. In each professional space, I did as my parents had always taught me to do. I wasn't loud or boisterous; I was quiet and focused. I worked twice as hard, often through lunch or after hours. I never took breaks. I didn't take PTO or vacations, dedicating myself to setting goals and going above and beyond in every job. I wanted to prove I was "one of the good ones," not wanting anyone to think negatively of me. The trauma I had internalized now made me focus only on making sure I looked like I was hardworking, industrious, and not someone who could cause any problems. Speaking out, speaking up, and being opinionated in professional spaces was just not an option.

As a college professor, the only place to be outspoken was my classroom. Faculty and administrative meetings were places to listen and keep my opinions to myself. I came to life in the classroom, wanting to be the mentor and supporter I never had. The knowledge of everything I had overcome as a college student made me so much more empathetic to my own students. For more than a decade, I taught mostly at community colleges and career colleges. Most were a short driving distance from where I grew up. Those students needed me the most, and I could be myself, laugh, joke, and share the story of my own upbringing and the challenges I'd overcome. I let them know they could rise above too. Of course,

I never shared that I had been arrested. But I let them know I understood what they were living through. I understood all too well.

By this point, I was more than aware of the studies conducted by the Education Trust[8] noting that most public flagships enroll a smaller percentage of Black students today than they did twenty years ago. According to the National Student Clearinghouse,[9] Black student enrollment has dropped by 13 percentage points. There has also been a steep decline in first-time enrollment among Black students, which sank nearly 19 percentage points across all sectors. Enrollment of undergraduate Black men at community colleges was particularly hard hit, falling 19.2 percentage points, compared to a decline of 9.0 percentage points for Black women.

And even if they were able to overcome the challenges to enroll in college, the Education Trust showed shocking disparities in graduation rates. There was a 17-percentage-point gap between Black (30.7 percent) and white adults (47.1 percent). This disparity persisted when examining educational attainment by gender. Slightly more than half of white women (51.4 percent) have a college degree, compared to 36.1 percent of Black women. The gap is even wider among men: 44.3 percent of white men have a college degree versus just 26.5 percent of Black men—a gap of 18 percentage points. While more Black women are earning college degrees, their economic prospects are still highly constrained by racism and sexism, and they're less likely to reap the full economic rewards of having a degree.

Because of my background as a college recruiter, I knew much of this before entering the college classroom. These students needed me, and it was my job to

---

8   Nichols, Andrew Howard. "Segregation Forever?" *The Education Trust*, July 21, 2020. edtrust.org/resource/segregation-forever.

9   St. Amour, Madeline. "Enrollment Declines Continue, National Student Clearinghouse Finds." Inside Higher Ed, November 12, 2020. www.insidehighered.com/news/2020/11/12/ enrollment-declines-continue-national-student-clearinghouse-finds.

show them that I wasn't unattainable, and neither was the professional success they were striving for. But I also understood the deck was stacked against them. Statistically, they were less likely to graduate and, even if they did graduate, they were less likely to be paid fairly in comparison to their counterparts.

The Education Trust also reports that Black women and Black men are overrepresented among those with some college and no degree. Just over 26 percent of Black women have some college and no degree compared to 21 percent of white women. Even more troubling: the proportion of Black men with some college and no degree (24.3 percent) is nearly the same as the proportion of Black men with a college degree (26.5 percent).[10]

According to the US Census, on average, Black women were paid 63 percent of what non-Hispanic white men were compensated in 2019. That means it takes the typical Black woman nineteen months to be paid what the average white man takes home in twelve months. That's even more shocking than the national earnings ratio for all women, 83 percent, as reported in AAUW's "The Simple Truth about the Gender Pay Gap."[11]

With all these disparities in mind, I approached my college classroom as a place to prepare my students, particularly Black women, who, without the shadow of a doubt, would face disparity. I informed them of the tools they would need for success. The main piece of advice I gave them was to be expert communicators. As a professor of English composition, American literature, and professional research writing, I knew well that it would be imperative that my students understand how to communicate effectively and succinctly.

---

10   Marshall, Jr., Nichols, and Del Pilar, "Raising Undergraduate Degree Attainment."

11   AAUW. "The Simple Truth about the Pay Gap." *AAUW*, 2021. www.aauw.org/resources/research/simple-truth.

Since I typically taught on community college campuses during my tenure as a college professor, many of my students were entering healthcare, business, criminal justice, and information technology. These were fields with no margin for error. And I was sure to warn my students of that. Everything needed to be documented and accounted for. I called it "receipts" with my students. And I knew that if I hadn't had my receipt, the outcome of my arrest would have been so much different. So, I always gave them the sage advice my mother gave me from her decades as a nurse. "If you didn't document it, it didn't happen." It was important for them to be able to articulate their thoughts, prove their points, and use credible evidence to guide their decision-making, especially in high-pressure situations they were sure to encounter in their day-to-day professional lives. The added burden of most of them being Black and Brown, speaking English as a second language, or being first-generation students was always an unspoken part of this never-ending tightrope act they would need to balance.

But outside of my college classroom, and even when I moved up into a director-level position in the Instructional Design department of my college, I was largely silent about the larger issues surrounding disparity. I had come to see it as the unfortunate part of the Black experience that I had no control over. I recalled my own experience as a college student and remembered that standing up for myself, even though it was the right thing to do, had still resulted in the added burden of an arrest record that I would carry for the rest of my life. It wasn't until I witnessed the murder of George Floyd more than twenty-five years later that I decided I no longer had any desire to censor or suppress my voice, regardless of my past experiences. I needed to be seen. But I also needed to be heard.

—

In thinking about who you really are, it's pertinent to determine how you were formed by your childhood experiences and environments; it's also helpful to understand the role of experiences you had in the self-determining time of young adulthood. There are particularly pivotal experiences that shape how you see yourself, your behavior, and your responses to the environments you navigate. Much of our early childhood may have been shaped by parents who told us to "be seen and not heard." They may have discouraged us from being the loudest in the room or speaking up too forcefully for fear of the emotional or even physical backlash we might face in a world that primarily does not look like us. Once we encountered that world, our parents' fears were often confirmed by the experiences we faced.

In my case, I learned that the person I presented as not only was unacceptable but could also be detrimental to my personal well-being. I learned to shrink from attention and tried to be as nondescript and unassuming as possible. I didn't like to get too much attention and tended to take my cues from others before deciding how to interact with them, rather than charting my own path for my behavior.

I was quick to second-guess myself in my interactions in predominantly white spaces, checking the volume of my voice, my facial expressions, and my mannerisms. I didn't want to appear too animated. I didn't want those I engaged with to feel threatened. So, I lowered my voice in meetings. I code-switched when talking to my boss, adopting a Valley-girl sing-song way of speaking, which I would abandon as soon as I left the building at the end of the workday. I minimized any hand gestures to emphasize a point when speaking or any other body movements that might indicate that I was "intimidating."

I also appropriated the majority culture's affects in my hairstyle, mannerisms, and style of dress. I had adopted this façade of professionalism when I navigated predominantly white spaces, programmed to believe they determined my success. I had learned to center white comfort and acceptance, using their viewpoints and mannerisms as the gold standard. I had internalized that narrative and had even begun to mimic them to ensure acceptability. Both my own authentic voice and the voices of my forefathers—mined from my diligent research on their history and lives when I first immigrated to America—became peripheral to my own lived experience, because my own experience had taught me that my authentic identity brought too much attention. I was the complete embodiment of *double consciousness*.

As an undergrad at the University of Florida, I took an African American literature course, the only course I ever had with a Black professor there, in my entire time as a student. It was in that class that I first read *The Souls of Black Folk*, by WEB DuBois.[12] I learned about the psychological challenge Black folk experienced of "always looking at oneself through the eyes" of a racist white society and "measuring oneself by the means of a nation that looked back in contempt." DuBois describes double consciousness as "a peculiar sensation... this sense of always looking at oneself through the eyes of others, of measuring one's soul by the tape of a world that looks on in amused contempt and pity. One ever feels his two-ness—an American, a Negro; two souls, two thoughts, two unreconciled strivings; two warring ideals in one dark body, whose dogged strength alone keeps it from being torn asunder."

He continues to say: "The history of the American Negro is the history of this strife—this longing to attain self-conscious manhood, to merge his double self into a better and truer self. In this merging he wishes neither of the older selves to be lost. He does not wish to Africanize America, for America has too much to teach the world and Africa. He wouldn't bleach his Negro blood in a flood of white Americanism, for he knows that Negro blood has a message for the world. He simply wishes to make it possible for a man to be both a Negro and an American without being cursed and spit upon by his fellows, without having the doors of opportunity closed roughly in his face."

---

12   Du Bois, W.E.B. *The Souls of Black Folk*. 1903. Reprint, New York: Barnes & Noble Classics, 2005.

Without comprehending what I was doing, with my actions I had begun to marginalize the identity I had fought so valiantly to learn, embrace, love, and understand. But even though I read about the phenomenon in college, it wasn't until much later that I connected DuBois' observations from a century earlier with my own experience.

My initial decision to delve within myself to unpack where the motivation for my own behavior had come from was spurred by the murder of George Floyd. Watching his life be taken, and witnessing the uprising across the country and even around the globe, made me take a pause to think about just how the internal trauma from my own arrest had affected me. I'll never forget where I was when I first saw the video. I was panicked by how much he had been dehumanized, and that it was obviously because of his brown skin. The victim-blaming narrative was a constant in the media, from how he looked, to his past actions, to his current circumstances. But it was clear to all of us that a change in any of those factors would not have had an impact on his final moments—a painful and horrific death at the hands of a police officer.

I also started to evaluate my own actions and how I had done everything in my power to avoid being the victim of racial profiling and a false arrest. But it slowly became clear to me that, regardless of my actions, I wasn't to blame. I also couldn't change the perceptions of others by turning into an alternate version of myself. Once I took the time to understand what had happened within me, I made a conscious effort to reclaim the self I really wanted to be. It was the self I assumed when I let my guard down at holiday dinners with my family. It was the self I assumed when I stepped out for a girls' night with my sorority sisters. It was the self I assumed when I ran around the park carefree with my kids. There was nothing unprofessional or wrong about this self. It was the self who was happy, confident, at ease, and comfortable in her skin.

First, I began to show that self in my interactions on social media. I became a self-proclaimed social justice warrior, taking to professional spaces like LinkedIn to share my feelings of disappointment, trepidation, and fear about what I had witnessed. I also began to speak about the importance of countering the narrative that "This isn't America." As a college professor of American literature, I knew those statements lacked an accurate understanding of American history. So, I started posting about exactly that. I posted about American history through the lens of an outsider—a Black British girl who had come to this country hungry to understand the beginnings and legacy of the Black American experience. I emphasized that it had begun long before enslaved Africans stepped foot on American soil. I explained how my knowledge of this history had transformed me for the better. I recounted how my experiences inhabiting predominantly white spaces had changed me again, but this time for the worse. I also documented my journey to recapture that confident and empowered self.

Then I began to embody that self in my conversations with coworkers, leaders, and the people I encountered on social media—all those who wanted to understand more about racial inequity and social justice. I decided that, if I was planning to advocate for marginalized Black folk, it would be hypocritical of me to show an alternative version of myself in my work of amplifying causes. I made a conscious effort to decolonize my mind, embodying and leaning into that authentic version of myself who had been dormant and untapped below the surface of my consciousness. When I did that, I found that I was able to tap into creativity, confidence, and empathy that I wasn't even aware I had. It was like a reservoir of spring water that was waiting for me to drink from it. I even became more confident in my personal relationships as I became more outspoken, honest, and verbal in my conversations. For the first time in both my personal and professional life, I felt truly free and happy.

Over the course of the past two years, I've spoken to dozens of Black women in all walks of life and careers. As my profile on social media grew to more than 100,000 followers, I was able to connect with Black women leaders at some of the biggest organizations in the country, like Microsoft, Nielsen, the City of Atlanta, JP Morgan Chase, and H&M. Many of them related to the idea of losing themselves to the persona that they were expected to present in the corporate spaces they inhabited. They often didn't even really identify with who they really were because it was vital to determine who they *needed* to be, as it was *that* person who would determine their level of success. And they had spent so much time code-switching, priming, and perfecting that alternate persona that they had totally lost their sense of self.

April Walker, senior vice president at Salesforce, explains[13] this feeling of navigating spaces in her more than two decades as one of the few Black women in leadership in tech at organizations like Microsoft, MetLife, and NBCUniversal Media. "There are so many women—whether they are early in careers or even some that are long tenured—[who] are still struggling to navigate the corporate space. How do we do that in a way that [allows us to be] authentic, but [also allows us to be] seen and...heard?"

"We are respected for what we bring," she points out, "but we are respected for the brilliance and the excellence we bring to an organization because we do impact the bottom line, believe it or not. We are staunch consumers of many of the products, in positions to either build or sell. I think about the political landscape. Look at what we've done. We put presidents in roles. So, when you think about that you have to be thinking, why do I not see more of us in the boardroom? Why do I not see more of us in the C-suite chair? I read this quote recently that I loved, and it said, 'If respect is not being served, you need to leave that table.'"

In speaking to the women who were most successful in their fields, I had the ability to learn so much, and one resounding truth became clear. It wasn't until they had leaned into who they really were at their core and uncovered their why,

---

13   Walker, April. "Inspiring the Next Generation of Black Women Leaders." Interview by Elizabeth Leiba. *Black Power Moves, EBONY Covering Black America Podcast Network,* March 1, 2022. ebonypodcastnetwork.com/black-power-moves.

i'm not yelling

based on their upbringing, life, and experience, that they were ultimately able to tap into their potential, while stepping into their true calling and success.

By uncovering how their experiences had framed who they really were, they were able to feel more comfortable in the boardrooms of Fortune 500 companies. This is because they appreciated their own worth and value and didn't question what they brought to those boardroom tables, classrooms, or national media campaigns.

One Black woman living her truth and reclaiming her personal identity while leaning into her personal narrative is Shonda Buchanan, an author and senior lecturer in African American studies at Loyola Marymount University. She was raised as a Black woman, but she also grew up hearing stories of her multiracial heritage. She traced the migration of free people of color in her family from the Southeast to the Midwest.

Ultimately, Buchanan's nomadic people endured a collective identity crisis after years of constantly straddling two, then three, races. The physical, spiritual, and emotional displacement of American Indians who met and married mixed or Black slaves and indentured servants at America's early crossroads is where her powerful journey begins.

"My book of poetry, *Who's Afraid of Black Indians*, came first," she explains.[14] "I compiled that book because I had been writing poems about my family, about heritage, about finding and reclaiming the Black Indian identity in a space of joy and self-acceptance, and just rebuilding my own sense of identity in opposition to what America had given me."

---

14   Buchanan, Shonda. "Who's Afraid of Black Indians?" Interview by Elizabeth Leiba. *Black Power Moves, EBONY Covering Black America Podcast Network*, March 17, 2022. ebonypodcastnetwork.com/black-power-moves.

I was touched by Buchanan's commitment to uncovering her true identity and how it impacted her ability to process trauma and understand where she really came from. Many of us are living through the same process of trying to figure out who we are and how our backgrounds, childhoods, and early experiences have shaped our current realities. And it's not until we have a sense of what our story is, and what it means, that we can find freedom in knowing who we really are—and a way forward.

Author Tracey Michae'l Lewis-Giggetts also discusses[15] the importance of that joy and acceptance in her collection of essays, *Black Joy: Stories of Resistance, Resilience, and Restoration*. "I think where it started for me was actually in grief. I had lost a family member to racial violence. A white man [walked] into a store in Lowell, Kentucky, and decided that two Black people would die that day. One of those was a family member—my elder cousin, and that sent me spiraling because I had been writing about reconciliation, racial justice, and all the things. But there's something that happens when it hits home."

"I experienced a severe health crisis for eight months," she explains, "trying to figure out what was going on in my body. I ended up learning [that], in addition to physical chronic illness, [there] was that trauma, that grief. The stuff that I was unpacking [...] through therapy was showing up physically. My therapist asked me a question that was really the catalyst for this book and my journey for the following two years, which was, 'What does joy feel like to you, Tracey?' I didn't know how to answer her."

She continues, "I was a forty-something-year-old and could not figure out what joy felt like in my body. I knew I'd experienced it. I could intellectually talk about it. But I didn't have a very embodied experience of it that I could recognize and call up. So, I began to do that work by really noticing when I was feeling joy and

---

15   Lewis-Giggetts, Tracey Michae'l. "Black Joy." Interview by Elizabeth Leiba. *Black Power Moves, EBONY Covering Black America Podcast Network*, April 24, 2022. ebonypodcastnetwork.com/black-power-moves.

identifying literally what it physically felt like in my body. [...] When my rage and my grief became so big—as it often does for us as Black people when we're seeing what we're seeing in the media and the news with everything—I had a snapshot of joy I could grab. It's not taking rage away, but it allowed me to... give myself grace and...self-compassion, which is one thing that I always talk about with us as Black folks. When we can extend more grace to ourselves and to each other, we then expand and make room for more joy to show up. Once I was able to do that, then I became really intentional about recreating those 'joy moments' in my life."

Tracey invites us to look at the way Black folks over time, on the course of "this four-hundred-year liberation project...wielded joy. How we've used joy as a strategy to stand in defiance of all of this dehumanization that we experience. But also, how we've used it to create, innovate, and how we've used it to heal ourselves. We've survived and then thrived as a result of being able to use our joy."

I advise Black women that much of the joy we lose is because we are always on guard. We always feel as though we must be exemplary, but in many ways that stifles our true potential. We feel as though we are the representative for all Black people, and most especially for all Black women. And we don't have the freedom that other races have to just be ourselves. We are careful, calculating, and not fully sure of ourselves, even though we seem competent and feel that way based on our attitude, experiences, education, and background. But that fully invested sense of trust in ourselves, based on living the truth of who we really are in professional spaces, just isn't quite there.

In my commitment to finding out who I was and to living that truth, I started asking myself critical self-reflection questions. I wrote the answers down, read them aloud to myself, thought about them, and started acting on them. I encourage you to do the same.

reflection questions

1. What is your favorite childhood memory? Who were you with and what were you doing?

2. When and where are you the happiest now? What are you doing, and what how does it feel?

3. What is your most valuable trait, and what are you the most skilled at doing? How does that make you feel? What trait do you like the least about yourself? What would you do to change it?

4. If you could do anything in the world without fear of failure, what would you do?

5. Who is your hero? What one question would you ask him or her?

6. When you were a child, what did you want to be when you grew up? Are you doing that now? Why or why not?

7. What are you most afraid of?

8. What are you most proud of?

9. If you could change one thing about your life, what would it be?

10. If you could wish for one thing, what would you wish for? What would it take for your wish to come true?

positive affirmations

1. My experiences have uniquely qualified me for everything I will accomplish today.

2. I am releasing old limiting beliefs about who I am now and who I have the potential to be.

3. I am happy and content at this moment.

4. I lean confidently into my most valuable traits and talents.

5. I am capable of successfully learning anything I don't have the knowledge to accomplish now.

6. I can accomplish anything I can dream of without a fear of failure.

7. I will overcome my fears today.

8. I am proud of the person I am today and the person I will be tomorrow.

9. I have the power to change my life.

10. I am attracting infinite abundance today and every day.

The answers to these questions helped me really start to clarify the areas where I had been holding myself back because I didn't want to step outside the constraints that I had created for myself. Many constraints were beyond my control. For example, I knew I couldn't change the behavior of others. However, there were also mental and emotional constraints that left me feeling as though I was walking on eggshells in every professional environment. By developing a confidence that I didn't only embody and embrace at home, but also embraced and stepped into fully when I went to work, I started to attract opportunities to myself that I never even dreamed were possible. I had considered myself a reasonably confident person, but I never stepped into my full power. By releasing myself from thinking in the back of my mind that I needed to be tentative and reserved, I allowed my full potential to shine through. This is because I started to really believe that anything was possible for me.

To reinforce that belief, I also started repeating daily positive affirmations based on the answers to my self-reflection questions to maintain my focus on the progress I was making in my internal journey. According to the Cleveland Clinic,[16] positive affirmations are phrases you can say, either aloud or in your head, to affirm yourself and build yourself up—especially during difficult situations. They're a way of helping overcome negative thoughts that can sometimes take over and make you doubt yourself.

Positive affirmations don't embrace a philosophy of toxic positivity. So, it's important to acknowledge hardship and make space for your feelings, while also calling on your ability to get through them. Being in a state of positivity takes practice, so it's helpful to repeat affirmations regularly and to put any skepticism on hold. When I first started using affirmations, I felt awkward. But the more I practiced, the easier and more natural it felt to use them. Another point that's pertinent to note is that positive affirmations don't necessarily have to be spoken aloud. They can also be repeated mentally. But it's important

---

16   Cleveland Clinic. "Do Positive Affirmations Work? What Experts Say." *Health Essentials*, December 7, 2021. health.clevelandclinic.org/do-positive-affirmations-work.

to keep them somewhere accessible to maintain consistency. They can be on notecards or in a phone app. Setting a timer on the cell phone to remind you to say them also helps with maintaining the routine of using them.

And finally, affirmations should be paired with action. I recommend looking at the answers to the questions and forming affirmations grounded in the past or present, but focused on what you want in the future. Repeating this type of positive affirmations helped me to visualize not only the person I was in the moment but also the person I was evolving to be. Putting those thoughts into the universe verbally created a tangible force that I used to help mobilize my actions.

You can't truly know where you're heading until you know where you came from. Both unpacking and analyzing the experiences that form your early impressions of the world around you and acknowledging the trauma and working through your responses are integral parts of being able to shed the baggage created by those emotions that are holding you back from stepping into your ultimate truth and power. Attempting to ignore it or downplay it is pointless because at some point you will experience a trigger that will bring all of that unconfronted trauma right to the surface. The most effective course of action is to determine what those pain points are and then to determine how each one has shaped the person you are today. From there you can determine who you want to be. That is your ultimate truth, and that truth is your life force and unstoppable power.

But to harness that power, we must first work through that trauma, understand it, acknowledge it, and reconcile it with how it shaped who we are today. Only then will we live in our truth without hiding from who we are, based on our past, and blaming ourselves for who we have become in the present. And much of the trauma we need to unpack is generational, passed down from our grandmothers to our mothers and then to us. Black women have been forced to endure unspeakable hardships throughout our American journey historically, since our ancestors first stepped foot on the soil of this country. Part of successfully navigating that journey is the ability to overcome the generational trauma we carry in addition to the present-day challenges.

It's critical to unpack and acknowledge trauma, rather than keeping those feelings inside. We also need to release any shame and not blame ourselves for negative experiences. We can't be held accountable for the past, especially when we're talking about and processing generational trauma. We also must give ourselves grace in understanding the reflex to protect ourselves due to our prior circumstances. But we also need to push ourselves to use our experiences in the past as a strength in knowing that we can overcome any challenges in the future.

Understanding who you are helps you to identify the reason for your "why," which will ultimately help you leverage the power of your story. From the shame of being a victim of racial profiling to the triumph of becoming a social justice warrior: that was my story. But everyone's story has power. Once you have harnessed the power from your past, you can use it to strengthen you in the present.

Living in your truth is the ultimate power, because it's magnetic. It attracts people to you that otherwise might not even notice you. Of course, it can't solve every problem. But it contributes to your own mental and emotional well-being. It confirms and embodies the mantra that you are enough. And by living in that way, when you step into professional spaces, you can shed emotional trauma and fear. This is because, as you walk in your truth, confidence, and power, what is for you will be yours.

Once we've established exactly who we are, it's time to step into that authenticity and to harness its power. In the next chapter, we'll explore the real power of being deliberate in our actions and unafraid of the consequences.

chapter 2

finding your voice

"There is no agony
like bearing an untold story inside you."

—Maya Angelou

Your voice can be a powerful weapon for the change you are looking for in your life. I will never forget reading the first volume of Maya Angelou's biography, *I Know Why the Caged Bird Sings*, when I was around eleven. The incident in her life that was particularly traumatic for her was learning that her voice had the power to unintentionally take someone's life.

Maya Angelou was the victim of a sexual assault at the age of seven. Her attacker, identified only by the name Mr. Freeman, had been dating her mother. When Maya eventually confided in her brother Bailey, he told Maya's mother. The man was arrested but only spent one night in jail. He was found murdered shortly afterward. Maya blamed the power of her words. The experience resulted in her refusing to speak for five years.

But as an adult, she would become the prolific writer, poet laureate, and civil rights advocate we all came to know. She used her voice intentionally and saved many lives, including my own. As Maya Angelou eloquently stated, there is agony in bearing an untold story inside you. Maya Angelou's story is even more fascinating because she told the truth about her experiences without fear of judgment. I was transfixed by her courage to not only experience everything but also talk about it unabashedly. At nineteen, she became the first Black bus conductor in the city of San Francisco. She traveled and performed in a production of *Porgy and Bess*. She was a call girl. She had a failed marriage and became a single mother. She traveled to Africa and worked with Malcolm X during the Civil Rights Movement.

Each experience was recounted exactly as it was—a milestone in the journey of her life. There was no regret. There was no shame. There was no silence after those early years. The first book in the seven-part autobiographical series about her life is called *I Know Why the Caged Bird Sings*. And the analogy admirably expresses the importance of self-expression in creating a sense of freedom. Words can be a lever to escape the feeling of oppression or entrapment. Maya Angelou used her lived experiences and the words that described them to create meaning. She lived up to her potential and empowered herself and everyone who would later read her works.

I must stop the urge to constantly tell my children to be quiet. Since I was very young, like many of us, I was instructed to stay in my lane and bite my tongue. As soon as we left the house, we were warned by our parents not to embarrass them. We were expected to behave in public spaces and not raise our voices to attract attention to ourselves. Granted, our parents had had their own experiences with the world that made them pass these lessons down. Unfortunately, this lesson has made many of us hesitant to be bold and outspoken in telling our stories. We have been reluctant to use the power of our voices and speak our own truths loudly and proudly.

Historically, the legacy and tradition of storytelling is a strong one across the African diaspora. And as for the descendants of kidnapped African slaves, their stories became a way to pass down the truth and preserve knowledge. But that truth was also a double-edged sword. In African tradition, stories related by griots and elders were passed down from generation to generation, telling about lineage, power, and a history of greatness. Here in America, being too bold in how you told your story and how you spoke to others that didn't look like you, or even learning to read and write, could get you killed. So that tradition and legacy were stolen. Reconciling generational trauma associated with that reality can be painful; however, leveraging the power of our true narratives is essential to reclaiming our power and finding our individual voices.

For me, healing the pain I carried from muting my voice meant becoming more intentional about how I talked to myself. I stopped telling myself "I can't." I just committed to giving my best effort every time. I also don't compare myself to others or engage in behaviors that lead me to telling myself I'm not good enough. How we speak to ourselves matters. What we say about ourselves matters. And I make a conscious effort to speak to myself and about myself with love. As a storyteller, I know that the story I tell myself is the most significant one. I must start with self-love—before I can even begin to claim my voice, use it effectively, or tell my story to anyone else.

My own journey started with healing the trauma of my past experiences by using my voice. I made a conscious and intentional choice to use my voice in a way that not only gave me strength but also empowered others. Once I had made the decision to speak my truth and not hold back in any interaction, I did that every single time. Whether it was answering a question in a leadership meeting at my college or posting an analysis of racial inequity in America, I decided that speaking my truth was a top priority.

When I used social media—primarily LinkedIn—to speak my truth, I grew from an initial following of a few thousand (mainly work colleagues and friends) to more than 120,000 followers in the course of about two years. Initially, after George Floyd was murdered, I was shellshocked by how traumatic it was to watch the event unfold on video. My first response was to retreat inward to protect myself from the anxiety I was feeling. But there was also a part of me that wanted to find a place to express all the hurt and pain that was bottled up inside, and LinkedIn became that place.

I posted about police brutality, racial inequity, Black history, empowerment of Black women, and even about my own personal experience of being racially profiled and arrested. I had never shared that story with anyone, even those in my personal circle. But telling my story was remarkably freeing. I was able to release the burden of shame I had carried and channel all the anger I felt about the injustice of the murder of George Floyd. Shortly afterwards, I was asked to write an op-ed piece for CNN about my own experience of being arrested. That article went viral with more than two million views on their website.

I posted daily after George Floyd was murdered in May of 2020 and, in those early days, many people, both on LinkedIn and in my professional circle, tried to dissuade me from being so vocal about racial inequity. I was warned that a professional networking platform was not the appropriate place for posting about social justice. My colleagues in higher education warned me that I would be targeted or shunned, and might miss out on potential career opportunities. But at that moment I didn't care. The only thing I wanted was speaking my truth and reconciling all the pain that was bottled up inside me. So, I committed to posting exactly how I felt.

Rather than repelling people and causing me to miss out on opportunities, I found that the exact opposite was true. In the wake of George Floyd's murder and the racial turmoil blowing up around the country, people were attracted to my message of disillusionment and confusion; they avidly followed my posts on LinkedIn. I attracted anywhere from one thousand followers a week to a thousand followers a day. By the end of the year, I had been named a LinkedIn Top Voice in Education; I had been interviewed by the *New York Times* and was the host of my first podcast. I would later go on to write an op-ed piece for CNN and be interviewed by *Forbes* and *Time* magazine. Next, I was tapped to start a podcast on the new podcast network launched by *Ebony*. All these opportunities came from people who had watched me tell my story and were attracted to its authenticity. The raw and uncut truth didn't offend people; instead, it helped them connect with my story and feel more invested in what I had to say.

I was amazed by how much more effective my messaging became, the more I strived to lean into my truth. I intentionally stopped focusing on how my truth might affect other people's feelings or perception of me, especially on this topic of racial injustice; instead, I focused on how to make my messaging as strong, credible, and convincing as possible. This novel approach was contrary to everything I had been doing all my life. I was always taught to worry about everyone else's feelings first. I never wanted to say anything that might make someone uncomfortable, so I watched how I spoke to coworkers and friends, or even my family members. In interactions both at home and at work, I walked on eggshells whenever I needed to express my true feelings, not wanting to assert myself too forcefully. But I was quickly learning that discomfort is a key component of equity work.

If we are to really move a discourse forward, we must expect a certain measure of discomfort. This is because people in the majority are asked to challenge beliefs they've held for a long time, sometimes since childhood. To speak up against disparity and champion the cause of social justice, I would have to speak the truth with as much authenticity and ferocity as possible; I would have to leave behind the notion that people's feelings were my primary concern. Doing this work caused me to be passionate about my message and dispassionate about the response to it. That same passion also became a natural response in advocating for myself. Telling the uncensored truth about my feelings, my background, and my experiences was like a cathartic healing elixir. It was wildly satisfying to express my true feelings without first worrying about someone's response to them. If my feelings were valid and appropriate for the setting, I made it my business to share them; I stopped censoring myself and practicing restraint. I made an intentional effort to use my voice rather than to be muted.

Restraint has always been considered a sign of strength, and much of this is historic. Black women, as the backbone of the Black community, have often learned that showing emotion can be fruitless and even dangerous to our own survival as well as the survival of our loved ones. To show anger, pain, or discomfort could lead to severe consequences. The generational trauma resulting from this practice is immeasurable. And the anxiety associated with constantly being so measured and calculated in not speaking our truth manifests itself in both our mental health and emotional well-being.

According to the American Psychological Association,[17] Black women are also simultaneously affected by racism and sexism and may feel under pressure to hide their negative emotions lest they fall prey to the "Angry Black Woman"

---

17   Pappas, Stephanie. "Effective Therapy with Black Women." American Psychological
     Association, 2021. www.apa.org/monitor/2021/11/ce-therapy-black-women.

i'm not yelling

stereotype. Black women are 1.8 times more likely than Black men to report sadness most or all the time; in addition, they are 2.4 times more likely than Black men to report feeling hopeless more or all the time. Black women are socialized to be strong and self-sufficient, a stereotype sometimes known as the "Superwoman Schema" or the "Strong Black Woman" role.

A study of 158 adult Black women[18] by Natalie Watson-Singleton, PhD, a clinical psychologist at Spelman College, found that agreement with the Strong Black Woman schema was associated with psychological distress, which was partially mediated by the women's perception of lack of emotional social support.

Black women are also judged more harshly than white women when they display anger or frustration. A recent study[19] led by Daphna Motro, PhD, a professor of management and entrepreneurship at Hofstra University, found that observers are more likely to frame a Black woman's anger in a workplace setting as internal to her, rather than due to external factors. As a result, the observers judged Black women as less capable leaders and as less competent performers.[20]

For fear of expressing emotions, and being labeled as angry or aggressive, Black women have historically employed silence as a coping mechanism. Women have faced—and continue to face—death for not remaining silent in the face of unspeakable abuse, both physical and mental, from the beginnings of the Black experience in American chattel slavery all the way up to the present day.

---

18   Watson-Singleton, Natalie N. "Strong Black Woman Schema and Psychological Distress: The Mediating Role of Perceived Emotional Support." *Journal of Black Psychology* 43, no. 8 (September 27, 2017): 778–88. doi.org/10.1177/0095798417732414.

19   Motro, Daphna. "Supplemental Material for Race and Reactions to Women's Expressions of Anger at Work: Examining the Effects of the 'Angry Black Woman' Stereotype." *Journal of Applied Psychology*, March 15, 2021. doi.org/10.1037/apl0000884.supp.

20   Pappas, 2021

In the Black community, there are a myriad of reasons we're urged not to express ourselves. We're taught to respect our elders and not speak back. We're taught to listen to our husbands because they are the head of the household. We're told not to question the teacher in school. We're told to keep our heads down, work hard, and not make any waves by drawing attention to ourselves at work. The rationale passed down from generation to generation is that hard work, compliance, and assimilation will be rewarded. We believe an outspoken woman will be shunned. When we are silent in the face of even the most brutal treatment, we are being told, just like in the past, that it is a sign of strength and resilience. But all the while, we ignore our own needs or wants and mute our own voices. As a result, we are slowly dying on the inside.

Author and anthropologist Zora Neale Hurston is famously quoted as having said, "If you are silent about your pain, they'll kill you and say you enjoyed it." And that profound quote expresses exactly the experience of many Black women as we navigate predominantly white spaces. We're often silent, avoiding conflicts, avoiding sharing too much about our backgrounds, upbringings, and personal experiences. We don't share our triumphs and we don't reveal our challenges. Instead, as Maya Angelou recited in "The Mask," her spoken-word adaptation of "We Wear the Mask" by poet Paul Laurence Dunbar:

> We wear the mask that grins and lies.
> It shades our cheeks and hides our eyes.
> This debt we pay to human guile
> With torn and bleeding hearts...
> We smile and mouth the myriad subtleties.
> Why should the world think otherwise
> In counting all our tears and sighs?
> Nay, let them only see us while
> We wear the mask.

We smile but oh my God
Our tears to thee from tortured souls arise
And we sing Oh Baby doll, now we sing...
The clay is vile beneath our feet
And long the mile
But let the world think otherwise.
We wear the mask.

So, because we have been conditioned to smile through our pain and bear it in silence, the trope of the "strong Black woman" continues to be perpetuated. We become unwitting participants in our own torture and oppression by not speaking up, not telling our story, or not correcting inaccuracies by those who take it upon themselves to tell our stories in our place. We become the victims of a never-ending cycle of misinformation that doesn't serve our needs and interests.

As someone entirely committed to learning about and amplifying Black history and culture, narratives, and stories of empowerment, I've always been drawn to the contemporary stories of Black women who stepped into their truth. I have also been inspired by the Black women who, throughout history, leveraged storytelling to empower themselves and advance the cause of Black liberation.

One such woman was Phillis Wheatley—the first African American female poet to be published, and one of the first women of any background to be published in the American colonies in 1773. Another one of my heroines is Harriet Ann Jacobs, who self-published *Incidents in the Life of a Slave Girl, Written by Herself* in 1861, after repeated rejections by publishers. This was an impressive feat for any woman of that era, let alone one who had spent years as a fugitive after being enslaved.

There was Ida B. Wells, an investigative journalist, educator, and one of the founders of the National Association for the Advancement of Colored People

(NAACP). In the 1890s, Wells documented lynching in the United States in articles and through her pamphlets called "Southern Horrors: Lynch Law in All Its Phases" and "The Red Record: Tabulated Statistics and Alleged Causes of Lynching in the United States."

And then finally, one of the stories that has always resonated with me was that of Sojourner Truth. She was born Isabella Baumfree in 1797 in New York State. Truth ran from her master in 1827 after he broke his promise to give her her freedom. She became a priest and an activist throughout the 1840s–1850s. She delivered her speech "Ain't I a Woman?" at the Women's Rights Convention in 1851, in which she questions the treatment of white women compared to Black women. Imagine my surprise when I started doing more research and found out that there are two versions of the speech. Even more surprising is that the version that most of us are aware of and is widely circulated is also acknowledged as being the most inaccurate of the two, since it was written and published twelve years after the original.

More bewildering is the fact that in the first complete transcription, published on June 21 in the *Anti-Slavery Bugle* by Marcus Robinson, an abolitionist and newspaper editor who acted as the convention's recording secretary, the question "Ain't I a Woman?" does not even appear. Twelve years later, in May 1863, Frances Dana Barker Gage published a very different transcription. She was a leading American reformer, feminist, and abolitionist, who worked closely with Susan B. Anthony and Elizabeth Cady Stanton, along with other leaders of the early women's rights movement in the United States. In it, she gave Truth many of the speech characteristics of Southern slaves, and she included original material that Robinson had not reported. Gage's version of the speech was republished in 1875, 1881, and 1889, and became the historic standard. This version is known as "Ain't I a Woman?" after its oft-repeated refrain. Truth's style of speech was not like that of Southern slaves. She was born and raised in New York and spoke only Dutch until she was nine years old.

I was stunned when I read this little-known fact. But it speaks to another concern that Black women face when navigating predominantly white spaces. I have often had my own words completely misinterpreted or misunderstood in leadership meetings. Oftentimes, I make a statement and the person appears to have heard the total opposite of what I said. Or sometimes people repeat things I've said in such a way that they are completely out of context or inconsistent with my intent. It's frustrating and exhausting. And as a college professor who's been in the classroom for more than a decade, I feel quite confident in my communication skills and ability to articulate points that I am making.

Just like Sojourner Truth, as Black women, we often have our own words twisted and used for purposes that we don't intend. This may be because there's already a bias against understanding us. This may also be because those receiving our messages are reinforcing stereotypes or tropes for their own purposes or agendas. That's another reason why it's so critical for us to tell our own stories. We need to reclaim our words and correct the attempts of others to purposely use our words and twist them to create their own narratives. There was a time when I would just ignore some of these "slip-ups," preferring not to "rock the boat" or appear too sensitive. I also often felt as though the effort "wasn't worth it."

But as I stepped more and more into my own truth, my goal became to ensure that I was reclaiming the power of my own story and voice. I then found that I was much less tolerant of my words being "misinterpreted." Words are a powerful tool. And the last thing I want someone to do is to take something I said and create more misunderstandings. So, to prevent that from happening, I would stop the meeting and clarify exactly what I said. I would ensure that I was understood before moving on to the next point. I didn't want to continue allowing others to twist my meaning or get into the habit of taking my words out of context. The first few times I did it, I felt uncomfortable. Someone had rephrased something I had just said in a meeting. It was the exact opposite of what I had stated. I interjected and just said, "For clarification, I actually meant—" and repeated the point I had just made. In that moment, there was a silence and then an acknowledgement. And I did that every single time it happened, which for me in the administrative offices of higher education is quite often.

Each time I did it, I felt less and less awkward. And even though it hasn't totally stopped, it happens less often. And I don't look at it as me making the other person uncomfortable. I am holding them accountable for listening with the intention to understand and for checking their own biases. And, whether they check them or not, I won't allow someone to create a narrative around me that is false, using my own words. A part of the process of empowerment in leveraging our narratives is also to ensure that the words are accurate. Just like what happened with Sojourner Truth, someone can take your own words and create an alternate version of your own truth.

When considering our truth, it extends to the fact that we're taught to ignore the inner voice that tells us we're tired, overworked, or underappreciated, or that what we're experiencing is a microaggression. The lesson about speaking back also applies when it's time for us to ask for a promotion or to negotiate a starting salary or a pay raise. I thought carefully about how to frame a conversation with my boss. I often refrained from telling the complete truth about how I felt because I didn't want to "rock the boat." At work, I would see initiatives that didn't make sense. But I didn't want to be seen as a troublemaker, so I didn't speak up. I didn't want people to label me as a "know-it-all" or an "Angry Black Woman," so I would often listen rather than express myself.

But one key point to keep in mind is that, no matter how much we conform, change our mannerisms, and alter our behavior, there's nothing we can do that will alter a perception of us that was formed long before this person even met us. And more than likely this bias has then been reinforced by their own perceptions throughout the years. Our attempt to reshape ourselves into a more palatable version of a Black woman is not going to do anything to change this negative stereotype they already hold.

We spend so much time softening our voices to fit what they think we should be. But the truth of the matter is that doing so will never work. It has nothing to do with how loudly or softly we speak. It has everything to do with our presence in these spaces. And the best thing we can do is to empower our voices and stay true to ourselves. We can shape our own narratives with the courage to tell our own stories about who we are and what we do. And the statistics show that, although we're just as qualified or even more so, we are underrepresented in the spaces we inhabit in corporate America and beyond. With that being the case, there is absolutely no reason for us to measure our words and not step into our truth in every space that we inhabit.

According to the US Census Bureau,[21] in 2019, on average Black women were paid 63 percent of what non-Hispanic white men were paid. That means it takes the typical Black woman nineteen months to be paid what the average white man takes home in twelve months. It's more alarming than the national earnings ratio for all women. Black women face a wider-than-average pay gap even though we participate in the workforce at much higher rates than most other women, according to AAUW.[22] Black women only account for 4 percent of C-suite positions, versus 62 percent for white men and 20 percent for white women, according to McKinsey & Company. These statistics are even more sobering when we consider the fact that among Black students in higher education, women are more likely than men to earn degrees: Black women get 64.1 percent

---

21   "A Supplement to the Simple Truth SYSTEMIC RACISM and the GENDER PAY GAP," n.d. www.aauw.org/app/uploads/2021/07/SimpleTruth_4.0-1.pdf.

22   AAUW. "Black Women and the Pay Gap." *AAUW*, 2018. ww3.aauw.org/article/black-women-and-the-pay-gap.

of bachelor's degrees, 71.5 percent of master's degrees and 65.9 percent of Black doctoral, medical, and dental degrees, based on data collected by AAUW.[23]

While we are second-guessing ourselves and telling ourselves we don't belong in spaces, we're more than qualified to be in the places we inhabit. Unpacking why we feel this way is complicated. Some attribute it to imposter syndrome, where we might feel less than adequate in spaces where we don't see ourselves represented. We'll talk about that more in the next chapter, as I tend to believe that the reason we second-guess ourselves is a result of the treatment we have received, not only over generations, resulting in generational trauma, but also in our own individual interactions in predominantly white spaces, arguably when we first enter them in the K–12 school system.

Historically, Black people in general and Black women particularly have been told that we didn't belong in predominantly white spaces. This has been the case since the foundation of America. So, when we were finally allowed to participate in society at the end of Reconstruction with the end of slavery, our participation was limited by segregation laws, policies, and practices that restricted our ability to fully engage in these spaces. The end of Jim Crow laws and the adoption of the Civil Rights Acts allowing us to live, eat, sleep and work in predominantly white spaces only occurred about sixty years ago. Despite the black-and-white photos and historical lens through which we view the civil rights era, it was relatively recent. With that being the case, despite Black women being highly educated, we are often "othered" and treated as though we are not as competent or qualified.

We all witnessed this in the recent nomination and confirmation of Supreme Court Justice Ketanji Brown Jackson. While it's true that the confirmation process is typically a contentious one, we witnessed an unusually irrelevant line of questioning and a demeaning attitude being levied against her, which was in stark contrast with the treatment of other nominees—particularly white

---

23   AAUW. "The Simple Truth about the Pay Gap." *AAUW*, 2021. https://www.aauw.org/resources/research/simple-truth/

men who have dominated the highest court in the land for more than two hundred years. She was more than qualified. And on the metrics that measure potential justices, she checked all the boxes. However, she was questioned and the skepticism of her competency from the predominantly white male Senate Judiciary Committee was glaringly obvious. She was clearly an exemplary nominee. But she wasn't being treated that way. She was being treated as though she didn't belong in that space. Ultimately, she answered every question and concern to everyone's satisfaction. But how many Black women without her stellar background, experience, and profile enter spaces where they are questioned, and then begin to question themselves? And that is another part of framing our own narrative. We can't be swayed by what other people think about us. We can't allow their perception to change our internal dialogue because ultimately, we can correct them, as Justice Jackson calmly did in each instance when they tried to mischaracterize her previous rulings or viewpoints. She knew she belonged there. So, her goal was only to ensure that the narrative about her background and experience was framed accurately.

Reframing the way I spoke to myself was a major hurdle—one I knew I had to overcome. I typically gave no thought to how I talked to myself. I questioned myself constantly, wondering if I was adequately prepared for each opportunity that came my way. I browbeat myself over the smallest mistake. I obsessed over being a model employee and put myself down if I didn't accomplish each goal set for myself. I didn't speak to myself lovingly or kindly. I didn't affirm myself or love myself. I was always my harshest critic. But I got to the point where I was so angry with myself and my own decisions that every thought was about how I couldn't do anything right.

My breakthrough came when I reached a breaking point and I felt like I couldn't get any lower. I was in a deep depression, and I was experiencing so much anxiety that every day my heart was racing uncontrollably. It was at that point that I started to take control of my own narrative and use my power to tell my own story. I started to be open and vulnerable with everything that was going on around me. I knew that I couldn't keep suppressing my voice because all the feelings I had inside were bubbling over. I paused to think about what I was saying to myself that was contributing to how I felt. I started talking to myself with love and acknowledging that my own feelings were valid. The more I started doing that, the more confidence I gained: I was going to be okay. I felt empowered to open up—to be authentic and honest in using my voice to express myself.

It was a two-way street: the more emboldened I became, the more people treated me differently because of my confidence; the more people were attracted to my confidence, the more I felt empowered to use my voice. When people ask me how I became so powerful in using my voice, I tell them that, one day, I just said enough is enough. The world was at the beginning of a global pandemic that was leaving an unimaginable amount of death in its wake. We had all just watched on television and social media the public execution of a Black man who'd simply resisted arrest. I had gotten to the point where I knew it would be unsustainable for me emotionally not to use my voice to talk about what I was feeling. I wanted to use it first for myself, as a means of coping, and then for others as a source of comfort.

Telling my own story accurately and authentically was the first step in reclaiming my voice. I no longer downplayed my accomplishments. I had grown up thinking that, if you bragged about yourself, you were a show-off or a know-it-all. But when I stepped into predominantly white spaces like college or the workplace, it was the people who spoke up about their skills and accomplishments who got the opportunities. I was taught to be humble and not brag when I did something well. But by being quiet about my wins, it gave someone else the opportunity to step in and take credit; they would talk about my project as though they had been the lead. Learning to control our own narrative is critical for our success both personally and professionally. It could be as simple as speaking up in a meeting or creating a brand on social media. Either way, it's important that people understand what you do, what your successes have been, what your track record is, and what you bring to the table; this is so that they can pay you, so you can replicate that success for them. Microaggressions will still happen, and opportunities may remain scarce. But, as my husband always told me, "A closed mouth doesn't get fed." Speaking up and being in control of our own story is better than someone else creating a narrative about us that is totally false.

When I started to embrace telling my story and expressing my true feelings to anyone who would listen, I found that all that anxiety, self-doubt, and hopelessness evaporated. It was such an amazing and freeing experience. Our words are extremely powerful. We need to be sure that, rather than being afraid of that power, we embrace and leverage it. Much like Maya Angelou, we may find it has the ability to not only elevate us in our present circumstances, but also to give us a degree of influence and opportunity we never imagined possible.

Another thing I learned is the importance of being truthful and authentic in my storytelling. This lesson was reinforced during a conversation with Seneca Dunmore, a motivational speaker earning six figures all over the country. She started out by just being authentic about telling her story, not just the triumphs but also the challenges. What she found was that, the more authentic her story was, the more women were drawn to her. They wanted to hear about her challenges and how she overcame them. The truth of the matter is that most of us don't have a straight path to any success. In our communities, we may have been taught to hide our struggles. But in this increasingly digital age of transparency, branding, and immediate gratification, it makes so much more sense to step into our full truth in all its glory, and even its heartache, because everyone loves the story of a champion, a warrior, and a conqueror. The story of the silver-spoon trust-fund baby? Not so much!

And I've met so many other women, from C-suite corporate executives to high-level military and government leaders, to women who work in some of the biggest media organizations around the country. They all found that, when they started leaning into their truths and telling their authentic stories, they were able to soar in both their personal and professional lives. Sometimes we're afraid to tell people about the challenges because we're afraid of being judged. We don't want people to think that we don't have it all together. We've been taught that we must be twice as competent. Therefore, telling anyone that we had doubts or stumbled along the way doesn't fit the coping strategies we've learned, even though that part of the story is just as valid as the success on the other side. And often it's that journey that draws people even closer to us.

That resonates with me so deeply because it mirrors my own personal journey in finding my voice. Rather than telling a carefully curated story, I began sharing a story that was true to myself and my real experiences, both the joy and the pain. I found that people were drawn to me in a way that never happened when I was so guarded. Of course, it's not possible or appropriate to be so transparent in every situation. But in many cases, people would rather see you as your real self. And if you are in a space that doesn't value that, then it's probably not a place where you want to be anyway. You'll be unhappy, and you'll eventually end up leaving. I started to tell the truth, not only to myself but also to those around me who needed to know. I didn't spare anyone's feelings or walk on eggshells. I kept it 100 percent, not only for them but also for me.

Today, many of the Black women we admire and emulate in business, media, and popular culture have been able to be so successful in large part due to their ability to overcome their circumstances to use their voices and create brands that have become synonymous with their personal stories.

Oprah Winfrey is a shining example of a Black woman who is amazingly adept at being transparent about her own personal challenges and struggles, articulating her story, creating a brand around that narrative, and creating connections that have leveraged her story and her name alone into a billion-dollar brand. Her name is one that most of us grew up seeing and hearing. We related to her story of coming from humble beginnings and growing to the height of her career in media to become the first Black woman billionaire, with a net worth of over two billion dollars.

She is best known for her talk show, *The Oprah Winfrey Show*, broadcast from Chicago, which was the highest-rated television program of its kind in history and ran in national syndication for twenty-five years. Dubbed the "Queen of All Media," she was the richest African American of the twentieth century, was once the world's only Black billionaire, and was the greatest Black philanthropist in US history. By 2007, she was sometimes ranked as the most influential woman in the world.

Oprah was born into poverty in rural Mississippi to a single teenage mother and later raised in inner-city Milwaukee. She was molested during her childhood and early teenage years and became pregnant at fourteen; her son was born prematurely and died in infancy. She was then sent to live with the man she calls her father, Vernon Winfrey, a barber in Nashville, Tennessee. She landed a job in radio while still in high school. By nineteen, she was a co-anchor for the local evening news. Her often emotional, extemporaneous delivery eventually led to her transfer to the daytime talk show arena, and after boosting a third-rated local Chicago talk show to first place, she launched her own production company.

By the mid-1990s, Winfrey had reinvented her show with a focus on literature, self-improvement, mindfulness, and spirituality. Credited with creating a more intimate, confessional form of media communication, in 2008, she formed her own network, the Oprah Winfrey Network (OWN).

Another woman who has stood out as a role model for Black women in leveraging her own story of triumph and inspiration is Michelle Obama. In 2020, Obama topped Gallup's poll of the most admired women in America for the third year running. Michelle Obama is an American attorney and author who served as First Lady of the United States from 2009 to 2017. She was the first Black woman to serve in this position, as the wife of former President Barack Obama.

Raised on the South Side of Chicago, Illinois, Michelle Obama is a graduate of Princeton University and Harvard Law School. In her early legal career, she worked at the law firm Sidley Austin, where she met Barack Obama. She subsequently worked in nonprofits and later became the associate dean of Student Services at the University of Chicago and the vice president for Community and External Affairs at the University of Chicago Medical Center. Michelle married Barack in 1992.

Obama campaigned for her husband's presidential bid throughout 2007 and 2008, delivering a keynote address at the 2008 Democratic National Convention. She delivered acclaimed speeches at the 2012, 2016, and 2020 conventions. As First Lady, Obama served as a role model for women and worked as an advocate for poverty awareness, education, nutrition, physical activity, and healthy eating. She supported American designers and was considered a fashion icon.

Beyoncé Giselle Knowles-Carter stands out in my mind as a powerhouse who controls and curates her own narrative extremely carefully so that she can determine exactly how her story will be told. As a singer, songwriter, and actress, she started by performing in various singing and dancing competitions as a child. She rose to fame in the late 1990s as the lead singer of Destiny's Child, one of the bestselling girl groups of all time. Their hiatus saw the release of her debut album *Dangerously in Love* in 2003, which featured the US Billboard Hot 100 number-one singles "Crazy in Love" and "Baby Boy."

Following the 2006 disbandment of Destiny's Child, she released her second solo album, *B'Day*, which contained the singles "Irreplaceable" and "Beautiful Liar." Beyoncé also starred in multiple films, such as *The Pink Panther*, *Dreamgirls*, *Obsessed*, and *The Lion King*. Her marriage to Jay-Z and her portrayal of Etta James in Cadillac Records influenced her third album, *I Am... Sasha Fierce* in 2008, which earned a record-setting six Grammy Awards in 2010.

Beyoncé released an eclectic fourth album in 2011. She later achieved universal acclaim for her sonically experimental visual albums, *Beyoncé* in 2013 and *Lemonade* in 2016. *Lemonade* was the world's bestselling album of 2016 and the most acclaimed album of her career, exploring themes of infidelity and womanism.

Beyoncé is one of the world's bestselling recording artists, having sold 120 million records worldwide. But she rarely gives interviews and is very strategic in the projects she chooses to affiliate herself with, remaining much of an enigma despite her dominant cultural influence. And that's what strikes me about the Black women who have been able to leverage their personal stories and brands so effectively. Each one did so intentionally without regard to the thoughts, opinions, or criticism coming from those who warned them that they might not be pursuing the most appropriate course of action. Oprah Winfrey created a talk show format that was totally different from anything that was out at the time. Michelle Obama pursued an Ivy League education and became an outspoken First Lady; she had her own career, accolades, and accomplishments very separate from her husband, with a very different approach in articulating her passions from any First Lady seen before. Contrary to most megastars, Beyoncé has remained an enigma; she rarely grants interviews and chooses only the projects that speak to her own personal brand of women's empowerment and Black pride.

The lesson to learn here is not to follow popular advice that suggests Black women must assimilate and only tell our stories in a way that makes sense to everyone. The truth is that our stories are unique, and those who relate to us will be drawn to us. Trying to appeal to everyone ultimately results in appealing to no one! So, therefore it's critical for Black women to own our narratives and to leverage them to articulate our backgrounds, knowledge, and experience; this will lead to more opportunities, promotions, or the ability to start a business. Being able to show exactly what we do and not dull the shine that we bring to every space we inhabit is an integral part of our individual success strategies in corporate America and beyond. This is not to negate the effects or ramifications of systemic racism or to imply that because Oprah Winfrey, Michelle Obama, or Beyoncé Knowles has been able to do it, then we "should" be capable to do it. What I am saying, however, is that if we don't take the time to develop our individual story, tell our story, and leverage our individual story, we will never know the potential of that story and what we might have been equipped to do if we told it rather than keeping it trapped inside us due to fear. Again, as Maya Angelou said, "There is no agony like bearing an untold story inside you."

In terms of brand recognition and representation, Black women are a hugely ignored segment of the marketplace despite their buying power. Our ability to leverage our stories thus allows us to capitalize on our brand management strategy, not only in the mainstream but also with other Black women. So many of us are not telling our stories and representing the fullness of what it means to be a Black woman. We can provide that representation for other Black women and provide unique offerings that create emotional as well as financial opportunities for ourselves.

According to McKinsey & Company,[24] a management consulting firm that advises on strategic management to corporations, governments, and other organizations, serving the Black consumer well is entirely possible for companies that take the time to figure out the needs of what others may dismiss as a "niche" audience.

Many products and services intentionally tailored to Black consumers have been immediately successful. Bevel, for example, is a brand of personal-care and grooming products created by a Black founder; the idea was born out of his own frustration that shaving products made for white men did not work for him.

---

24   Chui, Michael, Brian Chegg, Sajal Kohli, and Shelley Stewart, III. "The Black Consumer: A $300 Billion Opportunity." McKinsey & Company, August 6, 2021. www.mckinsey.com/featured-insights/diversity-and-inclusion/a-300-billion-dollar-opportunity-serving-the-emerging-black-american-consumer.

Launched in 2013, the company was acquired by Procter & Gamble in 2018 and is now expanding nationwide.

Similarly, Black women were long an afterthought for many major cosmetics companies. Singer and entrepreneur Rihanna saw an opportunity to create a brand centered on the needs of Black women. She launched Fenty Beauty, with a signature foundation product offered in fifty shades and designed for all skin tones. Garnering rave reviews, the company was valued at three billion dollars after just fifteen months. Rihanna has since introduced Savage X Fenty, a lingerie line celebrating body positivity, which was quickly valued at one billion dollars.

To gauge unmet demand, McKinsey & Company launched a proprietary consumer survey of 6,200 US consumers in April 2021.[25] Black consumers were far more likely than white respondents to say that current product and service offerings do not meet their needs, especially in personal-care products and services, banking and financial services, healthcare, and food. Black respondents also noted not seeing themselves in advertising and marketing campaigns, a lack of same-race business ownership, and a lack of company commitment to social justice.

In addition, Black women are the least satisfied with media representation, with only 18 percent feeling the media accurately portray women "all of the time" compared to 31 percent of Hispanic and Latinx women and 25 percent of white women.[26]

McKinsey & Company's analysis of the survey results suggests that Black consumers are willing to shift approximately $260 billion—about 30 percent of their current aggregate spending—to companies that can better deliver what

---

25   Chui et al., "The Black Consumer."

26   Keane, Megan, and Latha Sarathy. "Advancing Equality for Black, Hispanic & Latinx Women," SeeHer, August 21, 2020. www.seeher.com/wp-content/uploads/2020/12/SeeHerxDentsu_Whitepaper_PartII.pdf.

they need. They'll even pay up to 1.2 times more on average for offerings that are better suited to their needs and preferences. This could unlock another estimated $25 billion to $40 billion in net new spending. Together, these two figures add up to $300 billion in unmet demand. This is an invitation for innovative companies to compete and better meet the needs of Black consumers.[27]

Considering all these factors, there is a big opportunity for Black women to leverage their ability to create authentic narratives around the needs and concerns of Black women. There is also a huge market of potential clients, customers, listeners, and readers who are waiting to hear stories or buy products from women who look just like them.

During her more than a decade working with Nielsen, Charlene Polite Corley, vice president of Diverse Insights and Partnerships, has served as an advocate for more accurate representation of Black people in the media. "I am really proud of a release that we just put out that focused on the power and impact of diverse media owners," she says.[28] "Since 2020 with the murder of George Floyd, lots of huge brands and advertisers committed to spend more with Black-owned media. But the way that our data systems were designed weren't really to report on Black-owned ratings. So, we've been going through and trying to get our own house in order to gather folks up by ownership cohort and get an understanding of what that delivers to the marketplace, how they engage with audiences, and to provide some metrics about the power overall and then on average what you can expect from a Black-owned radio station in a market, [and] now 100. It turned into this great opportunity for Nielsen to look at the power of Black-owned media."

---

27   Chui et al., "The Black Consumer."

28   Polite Corley, Charlene. "Driving Representation in Media." Interview by Elizabeth Leiba. *Black Power Moves, EBONY Covering Black America Podcast Network*, March 14, 2022. ebonypodcastnetwork.com/black-power-moves.

She adds, "Another recent [example] was the report that we put out in December. In addition to television ratings or radio ratings, we also now measure representation on screen. So, not just who's in the audience with our ratings data. We also collect a lot of metadata behind the scenes of the program and who's cast and who directed. So, we can combine those data sets together and say, 'On broadcast television, Black men represented a 13 percent share of the screen time,' for example. And how does that line up with their presence in the population? So, we can get a sense of how different identity groups are showing up [in] most popular content on television across broadcast cable and streaming. [...] It allows us to use our capabilities to inform some of these really new goals that are popping up across the industry and to be more accountable to those because as the saying goes, 'What gets measured, gets managed.' And we believe that wholeheartedly! So, if we're not measuring and finding new ways to innovate and capture how people are thinking about identity or race and ethnicity, then we're going to fall behind. It's important to us to continue to reflect real people."

To that end, according to Nielsen's 2017 report titled "African American Women: Our Science, Her Magic,"[29] Black women's consumer preferences and brand affinities are resonating across the US mainstream, driving total Black spending power toward a record $1.5 trillion by 2021. At 24.3 million strong, Black women account for 14 percent of all US women and 52 percent of all African Americans. In the midst of data chronicling her steady growth in population, income, and educational attainment, the overarching takeaway for marketers and content creators is to keep "value and values" top of mind when thinking about this consumer segment.

Black women are trendsetters, brand loyalists, and early adopters, who care about projecting a positive self-image. They are playing an increasingly vital role

---

29   Grace, Cheryl, Andrew McCaskill, and Rebecca K. Roussell. "African-American Women: Our Science, Her Magic," Nielsen, September 2017. www.nielsen.com/wp-content/uploads/sites/3/2019/04/nielsen-african-american-diverse-intelligence-report-2017.pdf.

in how all women see themselves and influencing mainstream culture across several areas, including fashion, beauty, television, and music.[30]

During the two years I've been speaking with Black women actively on LinkedIn, I've met dozens of women who, using this knowledge, have been able to serve a market that has been largely ignored and underserved. Black women are now beginning to leverage their own voices and stories, to serve the needs of these women; in addition, they are also beginning to explain the power of brand awareness and management in leveraging our voices. One particularly effective example of a brand strategy powerhouse is that of Kanika Tolver, author and CEO of Career Rehab. Kanika is a certified AWS solutions architect and ServiceNow project manager. But her passion is helping Black women articulate their brands effectively in the workplace and pursue entrepreneurship if they choose. The strategies she shares[31] are extremely enlightening.

"It is really about being a brand and not an employee; shifting your mindset to understanding how you can be a brand even if you work in a company, even if you work in a nonprofit or government organization. But owning that you have ownership to the point that you can brand market and sell yourself into any job that you desire. So, a lot of people love the [concept of] dating jobs. I really focus on teaching people how to dump bad jobs and get into healthy career relationships. And I focus on them understanding that they don't need to stay in relationships that are no longer serving them because the job ends with benefits. When you identify what benefits you want out of that career relationship, you will be able to make more healthy career decisions and choices."

She continues, "I really like the idea of having career ownership. When you think of yourself as an employee, you only go to work and do what you're told.

---

30   Grace, McCaskill, and Roussell, "African-American Women: Our Science, Her Magic."

31   Tolver, Kanika. "Rebuilding Your Personal Brand and Rethinking the Way You Work." Interview by Elizabeth Leiba. *Black Power Moves, EBONY Covering Black America Podcast Network*, January 27, 2022. ebonypodcastnetwork.com/black-power-moves.

You don't go above and beyond to stand out. When you think of yourself as a brand you are saying, I have something unique for this organization. I'm a little CEO. I'm a little business. I'm a little consultant. And I don't even want to say the word 'little.' You are big, because we have to make the small things sound big in order to be a brand."

"That's why we go to Starbucks," she adds. "That's why we go to Chick-fil-A. That's why we buy tickets to go to Beyoncé's concerts, because they have learned to make the things that they're a subject matter expert at sound extremely big. So, when you shift your mindset to think of yourself as a brand, you can have unstoppable success. You don't feel stuck, because you know that if this is no longer serving you, you can move on to something else. [...] When you have an employee mindset, you have more fear. You have more anxiety. You have more career confusion. You don't have career clarity because you are subjecting yourselves to think what the employer thinks of you. And brands think highly of themselves. They work on themselves. They build themselves. So, if you are trying to build your brand within any professional sector, I highly recommend that you have a LinkedIn profile and an amazing resume. But have something unique that you offer that the other applicants don't offer, like a podcast show, like an e-book, like a YouTube channel, like a white paper, like a book, because they want to see that you know something so well that you can add value back to their organization."

These conversations served to validate my own thoughts about speaking my truth and telling my story without compromising. I started to unpack what my story meant and how to leverage my voice. Considering the answers to the questions on the next page helped me begin to frame my own narrative.

reflection questions ———————————

1. What is your true and authentic story?

2. How much of your narrative do you want to tell?

3. What is the importance of your story and who deserves to hear it?

4. How can you leverage your voice to feel more empowered?

5. What narrative are you telling yourself about your life?

6. How can you use positive self-affirmation to create accurate stories about yourself?

7. What stories are you embracing and which ones are you rejecting?

8. What is the importance of telling your story for others?

9. How can you scale your voice in ways that are effective?

10. What do you want the legacy of your story to be?

positive affirmations ————————————————

1. My story is powerful and deserves to be heard.

2. My truth is real and valid in every space I inhabit.

3. My voice is truth, and my truth is power.

4. I speak life in every interaction because life is in my words.

5. I value my story and so do others.

6. I embrace my stories that give me joy.

7. My story gives others strength and life.

8. My voice and my purpose are larger than me.

9. My story creates abundance and unlimited opportunities.

10. My voice is the legacy of my ancestors, and it will live forever.

In thinking about claiming my voice, four words come to mind: "It wasn't your fault." It wasn't my fault that people tried to silence me or take the power of my voice. It wasn't my fault that people spoke over me or contradicted me in my area of expertise. That doesn't make my voice any less valid. What invalidates my voice is not using it. My voice is my power, and I will always use it to claim that power. Overcoming doubt in the validity of our stories is a key process we will need to unpack. This will enable us to have the confidence to tell our stories to the best of our ability and to benefit us most effectively.

I continue the daily practice of affirmations to consistently reinforce the answers to the questions that framed my narrative and to remind myself of the power in my story. In claiming your power, begin to consider the small ways that you can tell your story and create a narrative for yourself that is accurate, authentic, and meaningful. You may start by speaking up in a meeting where you might otherwise have been quiet. As you gain more confidence, think about ways that you can continue to leverage your voice. Have you been thinking about asking for a raise or promotion but postponed having that conversation with your boss? Craft a story that explains why you deserve that promotion. That process can be intimidating, but often if we wait for those opportunities to come to us, they will never be forthcoming. Creating a narrative of competence and excellence puts us in line for opportunities and empowers us. Waiting for someone to recognize our greatness can lead to a waiting game that we may never win.

Another consideration is thinking about how to leverage your voice. I was able to do that using social media. The beautiful thing about social media is it gives you the ability to tell your story quickly, consistently, and authentically in any way you want. You can also scale your voice in a way that allows you to not only reach people all over the world, but to create a brand that expands outside the physical workplace and establishes you as a subject matter expert in your field. Social media can be as simple as a blog, podcast, YouTube channel, or any other medium where you can speak your truth. Using this as a strategy for empowering your voice not only creates a marketing tool for you to take advantage of additional opportunities, such as consulting within your field, it might also present other opportunities that you never thought of. Using social media to scale your voice also gives you the chance to explore your passions. I love to talk, but had no idea I would become a podcaster. By experimenting with that medium, I was able to scale my voice nationally. Our words are extremely powerful. We need to be sure that, rather than being afraid of that power, we embrace and use it. Much like Maya Angelou, we may find it has the power not only to elevate us in our present circumstances but also to give us a degree of influence and opportunity we never imagined possible. And in doing so, we will be connected with the network of other women, resources, and power that we can tap into with just the power of our own stories.

That opportunity to leverage and amplify my words, gain confidence in continuing to speak my truth, and realize that telling my authentic story not only impacted others but also helped me to connect with like-minded Black women first happened for me at the end of 2020. Ashanti Martin, a freelance writer for the *New York Times*, reached out to me to talk about an article she planned to write for the newspaper. She had observed several Black people, the majority of whom were women, using LinkedIn as a platform to post about social justice and racial equity in the aftermath of George Floyd's murder.

It was heartening to see that she had noticed this trend and that other Black women had also taken a stand in deciding that LinkedIn, a place for leaders in corporate America, professionals, and corporate organizations, was the perfect platform to engage in these discussions. The article she interviewed me for was titled "Black LinkedIn Is Thriving. Does LinkedIn Have a Problem with It?" It ended up on the front page of the *New York Times* business section. It also taught me that speaking my truth was more valuable than I ever imagined.

Lastly, as a historian, I can't understate the importance of storytelling to the Black community from a cultural perspective. Oral history was a part of our African heritage that allowed us to tell our stories, pass down family lineage, and create a sense of identity. The griot was the keeper of the stories in the village, who also served as an advisor and diplomat. Someone who can tell accurate and engaging stories and harness her power can mobilize and change the world. Embracing your voice and leaning into your truth, while leveraging and scaling it, can change your life.

chapter 3

imposter syndrome or imposter treatment?

"I still have a little imposter syndrome.
It never goes away,
that you're actually listening to me."

—Michelle Obama

I **remember first hearing that quote from Michelle Obama and thinking, "Wow!** Even Michelle Obama has imposter syndrome." And from everything she said about her background and experience growing up, it seemed perfectly reasonable. Imposter syndrome is defined as "a psychological condition that is characterized by persistent doubt concerning one's abilities or accomplishments, accompanied by the fear of being exposed as a fraud, despite evidence of one's ongoing success."[32]

Reading multiple stories about her upbringing, watching the *Belonging* documentary, and reflecting on my own experience as a Black woman allowed her words and her explanation about the impact of imposter syndrome to resonate deeply with me.

Michelle Obama was born Michelle LaVaughn Robinson on January 17, 1964, in Chicago, Illinois. She is the daughter of Fraser Robinson III, a city water plant employee and Democratic precinct captain, and Marian Shields Robinson, a secretary at Spiegel's catalog store. Her father suffered from multiple sclerosis, which had a profound effect on her; she was determined to stay out of trouble and perform well in school. By sixth grade, Michelle joined a gifted class at Bryn Mawr Elementary School. She attended Whitney Young High School, Chicago's first magnet high school, established as a selective enrollment school. The round-trip commute from the Robinsons' South Side home to the Near West Side, where the school was located, took three hours.

Michelle recalled being fearful of how others would perceive her but disregarded any negativity around her and used it "to fuel me, to keep me going." She recalled facing gender discrimination growing up, saying, for example, that rather than asking her for her opinion on a given subject, people commonly tended to ask what her older brother thought. She was on the honor roll for four years, took advanced placement classes, was a member of the National Honor Society, and

---

32   Merriam-Webster, 2021

served as student council treasurer. She graduated in 1981 as the salutatorian of her class.

Michelle was inspired to follow her brother to Princeton University, which she entered in 1981. She majored in sociology and minored in African American studies, graduating cum laude with a Bachelor of Arts in 1985 after completing a ninety-nine-page senior thesis under the supervision of Walter Wallace.

She recalls that some of her teachers in high school tried to dissuade her from applying, and that she had been warned against "setting my sights too high." She believed her brother's status as an alumnus—he graduated in 1983, before being hired as a basketball coach at Oregon State University and Brown University—may have helped her during the admission process, but she was determined to demonstrate her own worth. She has said she was overwhelmed during her first year. She attributes this to the fact that neither of her parents had graduated from college, and that she had never spent time on a college campus.

The mother of a white roommate reportedly tried to get her daughter reassigned because of Michelle's race. Michelle said being at Princeton was the first time she became more aware of her ethnicity and, despite the willingness of her classmates and teachers to reach out to her, she still felt "like a visitor on campus."

While at Princeton, as part of her requirements for graduation, she wrote her sociology thesis, "Princeton-Educated Blacks and the Black Community." She researched her thesis by sending a questionnaire to African American graduates. She asked them to specify when they enrolled and how comfortable they were with their race prior to their enrollment at Princeton; she also asked them how they felt about it when they were a student and since then. Of the four hundred alumni to whom she sent the survey, fewer than ninety responded. Her findings did not support her hope that the Black alumni would still identify with the African American community, even though they had attended an elite university and had the advantages that accrue to its graduates.

　　　　　　　　　　　　　　　　　　i'm not yelling

Michelle pursued professional study, earning her Juris Doctor (JD) degree from Harvard Law School in 1988. By the time she applied for Harvard Law, biographer Bond wrote, her confidence had increased: "This time around, there was no doubt in her mind that she had earned her place."[33] Her faculty mentor at Harvard Law was Charles Ogletree, who has said she had answered the question that had plagued her throughout her time at Princeton by the time she arrived at Harvard Law: whether she would remain the product of her parents or keep the identity she had acquired at Princeton; she had concluded she could be "both brilliant and Black."

So, in thinking about imposter syndrome and what it is, I had always framed my perspective based on accounts like Michelle Obama's and many others that I had read from women, and particularly from Black women. My interpretation was that imposter syndrome was the result of not feeling like I belonged in certain spaces because I looked so different from most people in that space. I assumed that the feeling was one that was internal and based on my own lack of confidence because the space didn't seem to be one that I could really excel in or, at least, one where I felt comfortable.

Many of us still struggle to fully, confidently, and authentically express and assert ourselves in our everyday interactions, especially at work and in the predominantly white spaces we navigate. There is a trauma that is holding us back. It may be a painful experience or interaction. Something has told us we are not good enough. That small voice stops us from speaking up in a meeting. It tells us we don't have the right to ask for a promotion or a raise. It tells us to avoid asserting ourselves in business negotiations. That small voice inside our heads stops us from listening to our real, authentic voices every day. Some people call that voice imposter syndrome, the feeling or fear that we will be found out as a fraud. But I had an experience a couple of years ago that led me to intentionally stop using that term.

---

33   Bond, Alma H. *Michelle Obama: A Biography*. Greenwood, 2011.

I had what I consider to be a life-changing conversation with Martin Pratt, publisher of *Philly Your Black News*. I was talking about how I have "imposter syndrome," and he stopped me mid-sentence. "Stop saying that, Liz." There was grave concern in his voice. "You're not an imposter, and you never have been."

That statement knocked me back on my heels for a minute. I started to ask myself why I had been using the phrase "imposter syndrome" to describe my trepidation when I stepped into predominantly white spaces and felt like I didn't belong or couldn't perform at the level I was expected to. Usually when people, particularly women and specifically Black women, say we have "imposter syndrome," we're talking about the dictionary definition—*something within us.*

I started to wonder why I had latched onto this phrase to explain and define my feelings. But the more I looked at the definition, the more I began to see that it didn't fit my experience at all. I'm not saying it's totally invalid, and maybe it applies to other people. But it didn't apply to me, because I knew I was accomplished. I had the background and experience to get the job done. I didn't feel like I would be exposed as a fraud at all! And I also started to explore my feelings in those spaces. Was it really me who had persistent doubts—or did people who didn't look like me and were the majority in those places express doubts in my ability either explicitly or implicitly? It became clear that, in fact, my malaise came *from outside of me*, from the hostile spaces I stepped into.

Michelle Obama, for example, excelled in every academic environment, starting in sixth grade when she enrolled in the gifted program. She attended a magnet high school. But despite her early academic success, she was fearful of how others would perceive her based on where she was from and because she didn't look like them. And that fear was reinforced when some of her teachers in high school tried to dissuade her from applying to Princeton, warning her against what she described as "setting my sights too high." However, she graduated from the undergraduate program in sociology and earned her JD from Harvard University.

Much like Michelle Obama, I understood the assignment in every space I inhabited. And I always got an A+. I performed over and above others who didn't look like me and were mediocre. But they still managed to get the promotions and raises that I wasn't "qualified" to receive. I had to endure being spoken over, having to recite my resume to convince people to listen to my ideas and take me seriously. Then I still had to perform twice as well to prove my worth. I worked through lunch and never left the office early because I didn't want anyone to say the Black girl was "lazy."

After putting my experience in context, I decided to stop referring to myself as having "imposter syndrome." The truth of the matter was that I didn't feel like an imposter. I had been *treated* like one. I had internalized the message that I was a fraud when I was Black girl magic personified! Not referring to myself as having "imposter syndrome" and walking in the power that, as my friend said, I wasn't one (and never had been) changed my life. It's not to say that I don't have fears, but I am aware of my strengths and my power. And the things I don't know, I can work on to get better. However, I know that the statistics about imposter syndrome as a phenomenon that many women feel they are experiencing are staggering. The effects of this feeling are real, regardless of my claim that it's not our own feelings that lead to imposter syndrome. It's the fact that we are treated like imposters that leads to these feelings of doubt when we navigate predominantly white spaces.

But it's easy to see why many people, especially Black women, haven't made that distinction. According to the American Psychological Association,[34] Imposter syndrome was first described by psychologists Suzanne Imes, PhD, and Pauline Rose Clance, PhD, in the 1970s. They observed that this phenomenon they had identified occurs among high achievers who are unable to internalize and accept

---

34 Clance, Pauline Rose, and Suzanne Ament Imes. "The Imposter Phenomenon in High Achieving Women: Dynamics and Therapeutic Intervention." *Psychotherapy: Theory, Research & Practice* 15, no. 3 (1978): 241–47. doi.org/10.1037/h0086006.

their success. They often attribute their accomplishments to luck rather than to ability, and fear that others will eventually unmask them as a fraud.[35]

When Clance and Imes first described the imposter phenomenon (sometimes called imposter syndrome), they thought it was unique to women. Since then, a variety of research on the topic has revealed that men, too, can have the unenviable experience of feeling like frauds, according to a recent research review.[36]

According to Imes, many people who feel like imposters grew up in families that placed a big emphasis on achievement. In particular, parents who send mixed messages—alternating between over-praise and criticism—can increase the risk of future fraudulent feelings.

A 2013 study by researchers at the University of Texas at Austin surveyed ethnic minority college students and found that Asian-Americans were more likely than African Americans or Latino-Americans to experience imposter feelings. Interestingly, the researchers also found that imposter feelings more strongly predicted mental health problems than did stress related to one's minority status.[37]

Some of the additional causes cited by psychologists for imposter syndrome include personality types, like low-efficacy, perfectionism, and neuroticism.

---

35   Weir, Kirsten. "Feel like a Fraud?" American Psychological Association, 2013. www.apa. org/gradpsych/2013/11/fraud.

36   Coverdale, John. "Behavioral Sciences: An International, Open-Access, Peer Reviewed Journal." *Behavioral Sciences* 1, no. 1 (February 22, 2011): 1–3. doi.org/10.3390/ behavsci1010001.

37   McClain, Shannon, Samuel T. Beasley, Bianca Jones, Olufunke Awosogba, Stacey Jackson, and Kevin Cokley. "An Examination of the Impact of Racial and Ethnic Identity, Impostor Feelings, and Minority Status Stress on the Mental Health of Black College Students." *Journal of Multicultural Counseling and Development*, 44, no. 2 (April 2016): 101–17. doi. org/10.1002/jmcd.12040.

There is also some speculation that imposter syndrome and social anxiety may overlap. A person with social anxiety disorder (SAD) may feel as though they don't belong in interpersonal or performance situations.[38]

The common thread in all of the research about imposter syndrome and how it originates is the idea that its root cause is internal. And this is where I started to feel the disconnect after reviewing all the research. With its roots in clinical psychology, scholars have predominantly depicted the imposter phenomenon as a personality trait that originates within the individuals who experience imposter feelings.[39] This focus on the individual level of analysis is most likely the result of the fact that the phenomenon is reflective of a negative and critical self-concept[40] and negatively affects the individuals who experience it.[41]

Although it is estimated that 70 percent of people will undergo at least one episode of this phenomenon in their lives, most people who have been documented to experience it are women or members of historically marginalized groups.[42]

---

38   Cuncic, Arlin. "What Is Imposter Syndrome?" *Verywell Mind*, May 1, 2020. www.verywellmind.com/imposter-syndrome-and-social-anxiety-disorder-4156469.

39   Feenstra, Sanne, Christopher T. Begeny, Michelle K. Ryan, Floor A. Rink, Janka I. Stoker, and Jennifer Jordan. "Contextualizing the Impostor 'Syndrome.'" *Frontiers in Psychology* 11 (November 13, 2020). doi.org/10.3389/fpsyg.2020.575024.

40   Clance and Imes, "The Imposter Phenomenon."

41   Sonnak, Carina, and Tony Towell. "The Impostor Phenomenon in British University Students: Relationships between Self-Esteem, Mental Health, Parental Rearing Style and Socioeconomic Status." *Personality and Individual Differences* 31, no. 6 (October 2001): 863–74. doi.org/10.1016/s0191-8869(00)00184-7.

42   Cuncic, "What Is Impostor Syndrome?"

For example, because of the stereotype of the "good" leader possessing predominantly masculine traits,[43] women are often depicted as lacking leadership qualities (i.e., they are stereotypically perceived as communal and warm), while men are portrayed as having a more natural fit for leadership positions (i.e., they are stereotypically perceived as agentic and assertive☺).[44] In response to these gender and leadership stereotypes, research suggests that a woman may feel insecure and out of place if she achieves such a leadership position. This is because these pervasive stereotypes have consistently signaled, both directly and indirectly, that she would not be fit for such a position.[45]

First, studies indicate that a woman's awareness of such stereotypes can trigger her to feel like an imposter.[46] This may also help explain inconsistencies in the current literature regarding gender differences in imposter feelings (with some studies showing that women experience more imposter feelings, while other

43   Powell, Gary N., D. Anthony Butterfield, and Jane D. Parent. "Gender and Managerial Stereotypes: Have the Times Changed?" *Journal of Management* 28, no. 2 (April 2002): 177–93. doi.org/10.1177/014920630202800203.

44   Heilman, Madeline E. "Description and Prescription: How Gender Stereotypes Prevent Women's Ascent up the Organizational Ladder." *Journal of Social Issues* 57, no. 4 (January 2001): 657–74. doi.org/10.1111/0022-4537.00234.

45   Haynes, Michelle C., and Madeline E. Heilman. "It Had to Be You (Not Me)!" *Personality and Social Psychology Bulletin* 39, no. 7 (May 7, 2013): 956–69. doi. org/10.1177/0146167213486358.

      Heilman, Madeline E. "Gender Stereotypes and Workplace Bias." *Research in Organizational Behavior* 32, no. 32 (January 2012): 113–35. doi.org/10.1016/j. riob.2012.11.003.

46   Cokley K., Awad G., Smith L., Jackson S., Awosogba O., Hurst A., et al. (2015). "The Roles of Gender Stigma Consciousness, Impostor Phenomenon and Academic Self-Concept in the Academic Outcomes of Women and Men." *Sex Roles* 73 414-426. 10.1007/s11199-015-0516-7

studies failed to find gender differences),[47] as reasoning suggests that women would only feel like imposters in contexts that signal that they are so.

Likewise, certain ethnic minorities are stereotyped as being unintelligent, lazy, and/or underachieving.[48] In response to such negative portrayals of their group, ethnic minority students are likely to worry that their admission to, for instance, a prestigious university is the outcome of luck, instead of something they deserve.

In line with such reasoning, research examining imposter feelings among ethnic minority students indeed showed that students who reported being racially discriminated against were more likely to feel like imposters.[49] Overall, this suggests that, at the societal level, the group that someone belongs to, and the

---

47   Bravata D. M., Watts S. A., Keefer A. L., Madhusudhan D. K., Taylor K. T., Clark D. M., et al. (2019). "Prevalence, Predictors, and Treatment of Impostor Syndrome: A Systematic Review." *Journal of General Internal Medicine*. 35 1252–1275. 10.1007/s11606-019-05364-1

48   Reyna C. (2000). "Lazy, Dumb, or Industrious: When Stereotypes Convey Attribution Information in the Classroom." *Educational Psychology Review*. 12 85–110. 10.1023/A:1009037101170

      Reyna C. (2008). "Ian Is Intelligent but Leshaun Is Lazy: Antecedents and Consequences of Attributional Stereotypes in the Classroom." *European Journal of Psychology of Education. Educ*. 23 439–458. 10.1007/BF03172752

49   Austin C. C., Clark E. M., Ross M. J., Taylor M. J. (2009). "Impostorism as a Mediator between Survivor Guilt and Depression in a Sample of African American College Students." *College Student Journal*. J. 43 1094–1109.

      Cokley K., Smith L., Bernard D., Hurst A., Jackson S., Stone S., et al. (2017). "Impostor Feelings as a Moderator and Mediator of the Relationship between Perceived Discrimination and Mental Health among Racial/Ethnic Minority College Students." *Journal of Counseling Psychology*. 64 141–154. 10.1037/cou0000198

      Bernard D. L., Hoggard L. S., Neblett E. W., Jr. (2018). "Racial Discrimination, Racial Identity, and Impostor Phenomenon: A Profile Approach." *Cultural Diversity and Ethnic Minority Psychology*. 24 51–61. 10.1037/cdp0000161

portrayal of those groups in society, play an instrumental role in triggering individuals' imposter feelings.[50]

It's the classic example of the chicken or the egg. Which came first? Which one you choose may very likely have a lot to do with your experiences and beliefs—science versus religion, for instance—and your exposure to the validity of each theory. But I, like many of us, can't say I ever experienced feeling out of place or less than competent until I entered environments where most of the people did not look like me. For many of my formative years, I felt like I was intellectually superior and more than competent. It wasn't until I entered environments where I felt significantly different in race, gender, and economic background that those feelings of confidence began to slowly melt away.

In addition to the broader societal context, research from social and organizational psychology suggests that features within the more immediate institutional context (e.g., within corporate organizations or educational or government institutions) play an active role in shaping imposter feelings as well.

Here, women and ethnic minority group members are, for instance, more or less likely to occupy particular professions (e.g., they are underrepresented in surgery, but overrepresented in nursing), particular roles within an organization (e.g., they are underrepresented in information technology, but overrepresented in human resources), and particular levels of organizational hierarchies (e.g., they are underrepresented in leadership positions, but overrepresented at more junior levels).[51]

---

50   Feenstra et al., 2020

51   Catalyst. "Quick Take: Women in the Workforce." *Catalyst,* February 11, 2021. www.catalyst.org/research/women-in-the-workforce-global.

Moreover, they often lack role models and are paid less for the work they do.[52] Research suggests that such a lack of representation and lower compensation, in turn, elicit doubts about one's suitability for these occupations and positions.[53]

Finally, social psychological research suggests that how people are treated by self-relevant others is an important precursor to imposter feelings. This is because individuals' everyday interactions are laced with significant social evaluative cues, conveying whether others see them as a person of value and worth.[54]

These social evaluative cues ultimately guide individuals' appraisals of their own self-worth, and thus shape their self-esteem and sense of being worthy or deserving of their "place" within that group or context.[55] In traditionally white, male-dominated occupations, for example, female and ethnic minority employees are often perceived and treated differently (e.g., they are less often

52   Catalyst, "Quick Take: Women in the Workforce."

      Lyness, Karen S., and Donna E. Thompson. "Climbing the Corporate Ladder: Do Female and Male Executives Follow the Same Route?" *Journal of Applied Psychology* 85, no. 1 (2000): 86–101. doi.org/10.1037/0021-9010.85.1.86.

53   Peters, Kim, S. Alexander Haslam, Michelle K. Ryan, and Miguel Fonseca. "Working with Subgroup Identities to Build Organizational Identification and Support for Organizational Strategy." *Group & Organization Management* 38, no. 1 (January 4, 2013): 128–44. doi.org/10.1177/1059601112472368.

54   Huo, Yuen J., and Kevin R. Binning. "Why the Psychological Experience of Respect Matters in Group Life: An Integrative Account." *Social and Personality Psychology Compass* 2, no. 4 (July 2008): 1570–85. doi.org/10.1111/j.1751-9004.2008.00129.x.

      Smith, Heather J., Tom R. Tyler, Yuen J. Huo, Daniel J. Ortiz, and E. Allan Lind. "The Self-Relevant Implications of the Group-Value Model: Group Membership, Self-Worth, and Treatment Quality." *Journal of Experimental Social Psychology* 34, no. 5 (September 1998): 470–93. doi.org/10.1006/jesp.1998.1360.

55   Cohen, Ronald L., E. Allan Lind, and Tom R. Tyler. "The Social Psychology of Procedural Justice." *Contemporary Sociology* 18, no. 5 (September 1989): 758. doi.org/10.2307/2073346.

sought out for advice, or included in work-related discussions).[56] Such subtle everyday oversights communicate that these employees' ideas, knowledge, and insights are valued less than those of other employees. This can in turn perpetuate issues of confidence and engagement at work.[57]

This research and accompanying context from psychological studies directly relates back to the examples given by Michelle Obama, who is often cited as someone who "suffered" from imposter syndrome. Given the role played by external factors such as stereotypes and social evaluative cues, conveying her value and worth, I'd say that Michelle Obama was subjected to *imposter treatment*. As I pondered some of her difficult interactions, rooted in gender and racial discrimination, I realized that her self-doubt was not the indication of a personality flaw or some internal force stemming from her family upbringing; it was not a sign of social anxiety disorder. Michelle Obama was never an imposter. And, as my friend had so accurately reminded me, neither was I. Michelle and I had simply been *treated* like imposters in the predominantly white spaces we inhabited and navigated. This treatment was what led to anxiety and trepidation, and to reduced confidence.

Regardless of the cause, the effects of what has been labeled imposter syndrome are quite real. For me, it led to feelings of inadequacy, confusion, and anxiety. According to psychologists, these feelings eventually worsen anxiety and may lead to depression. People who experience imposter syndrome also tend not to

---

56   Begeny, C. T., M. K. Ryan, C. A. Moss-Racusin, and G. Ravetz. "In Some Professions, Women Have Become Well Represented, yet Gender Bias Persists—Perpetuated by Those Who Think It Is Not Happening." *Science Advances* 6, no. 26 (June 1, 2020): eaba7814. doi.org/10.1126/sciadv.aba7814.

     Dovidio, John F, Nancy Evans, and Richard B Tyler. "Racial Stereotypes: The Contents of Their Cognitive Representations." *Journal of Experimental Social Psychology* 22, no. 1 (January 1986): 22–37. doi.org/10.1016/0022-1031(86)90039-9.

57   Holleran, Shannon E., Jessica Whitehead, Toni Schmader, and Matthias R. Mehl. "Talking Shop and Shooting the Breeze." *Social Psychological and Personality Science* 2, no. 1 (August 13, 2010): 65–71. doi.org/10.1177/1948550610379921.

i'm not yelling

talk about how they are feeling with anyone and struggle in silence.[58] This cycle can quickly become exhausting and has plenty of negative implications on not only your career, but your health, well-being, and personal relationships.[59]

"Imposter syndrome contributes to psychological distress, continued self-monitoring, increased self-doubt and persistent fears of failure," psychologist Dr. Audrey Ervin says. [60] "It can negatively impact careers because people may overproduce to prove that they are capable. This can lead to burnout and ultimately be counterproductive. People may also miss opportunities because they do not feel worthy or capable, despite being quite competent. Imposter syndrome can negatively impact relationships when a family member prioritizes career success over time with families or children. Partners and families can suffer when someone spends too much time trying to prove themselves in a professional capacity to the detriment of their personal lives."

So, for Black women who are already dealing with systemic disparities, as well as institutional marginalization in organizations and social psychological interactions that may be unhealthy, invalidating, or even toxic, carrying around an additional stigma of imposter syndrome is a burden that needs to be released. Rather than being pathologized as an internal lack of confidence, self-sabotage, or paranoia, it needs to be recognized as an externally caused symptom of a society that, historically, has systematically excluded Black women from many spaces—a society that has told Black women, either implicitly or explicitly, that we don't belong in those places, that we are not as worthy as those who are in the majority. Over generations, and up to the present day, this has had a compounding effect, resulting in a lack of representation in those places. We

58   Cuncic, "What Is Impostor Syndrome?"

59   Page, Danielle. "How Impostor Syndrome Is Holding You Back at Work." NBC News. NBC News, October 26, 2017. www.nbcnews.com/better/health/how-impostor-syndrome-holding-you-back-work-ncna814231.

60   Page, "How Impostor Syndrome Is Holding You Back."

are not and have never been imposters. And most of us never felt like imposters until we entered those spaces.

That realization was a lightbulb moment for me. There was absolutely nothing wrong with me. My fear and anxiety were not some self-imposed doubts that I needed to "work through." I started adopting the attitude that if I was in a space, then I belonged there; I had a right to be there, and I would stay there and be successful for as long as felt right for me. And the more I told myself that, the less trepidation I felt every time I entered a place where no one looked like me. Even if others weren't welcoming or nurturing toward me, I looked at their actions as their own personal failure—not as an indication of a lack of competence on my part. After all, whenever I entered a space, it was because I had been invited into it by someone in charge. I hadn't simply shown up without warning! I had the required qualifications to be there. I had the education and credentials. So, I began to realize that if anyone mistreated me, that was their problem and certainly not mine. I would still hold my head up high and be confident in my interaction. Their opinion of my worthiness or their attitude toward my presence didn't change the fact that I truly did belong there. I also didn't allow any negative feedback to enter my mind in future interactions. Each space was a brand-new opportunity that I entered knowing I belonged and was there to fulfill my purpose.

But I still am a work in progress when it comes to stepping into my power and not doubting myself. It takes consistent checking of my own thought patterns and behaviors to ensure that I'm not downplaying my abilities; that I'm being confident in the skills that I have, while working on those I need to improve. On a recent call with a speakers' bureau, we started strategizing about speaking engagements and areas of interest for me to potentially hold talks for corporate clients. I explained that I had done at least a dozen talks over the past year for big organizations like Reddit, Forever 21, and Zelle on social justice, Black history, and racial equity. "But I'm not an expert in DEI," I said after rattling off all my experience. The owner of the speakers' bureau, a middle-aged white man who represents clients like Common, Taraji P, Henson, and Chuck D, immediately paused the conversation.

"Wait a minute," he said. "You *are* a DEI expert. Aside from all the speaking you've done on this topic for huge corporate organizations, you also have your own lived experience. That's priceless."

I stopped for a moment. "You're right," I responded.

So, there's another example. Despite having given presentations about my own perspectives on race all across America, I was still checking out and letting him know that I wasn't really "qualified." That kind of self-talk is something to address and recognize so we can change it. And it doesn't mean that we should be confident about topics we have no knowledge of; it means that we should be aware of our strengths, lean into them, and commit to continuing to grow, learn, and develop. This is instead of checking out and counting ourselves out before we've even started.

I recently saw a post on social media that captured this phenomenon so concisely. The number of women who expressed surprise that they had never even considered the harm this term was causing was telling: It showed how pervasive the use of "imposter syndrome" is, and how much it is affecting Black women's perceptions of themselves.

The viral tweet was posted on April 13, 2022, by Juana Hollingsworth, MSW, a graduate research assistant at Morgan State University and a Diversity Education fellow at Johns Hopkins University. Her quote said that, as of that day, she was no longer using the term "imposter syndrome." Her rationale for discontinuing its use fell so completely in line with everything I had been thinking in the previous year.

"In reality, the root of this fraud feeling is a result of systemic bias & exclusion! & rather than naming that, society a.k.a. the academy found another way to cover it up & name the experiences of marginalized communities that places blame on the person rather than the system."

Claiming imposter syndrome as a "thing" that you have can serve as a limiting belief rather than providing context for how you feel. In my opinion and experience, when you identify the so-called "imposter syndrome" as a personal challenge, something to overcome within yourself, it leads you to accept this "syndrome" as a feeling that diminishes your self-worth. It also creates a pathology out of a natural reaction to being mistreated. It blames the victim of the affronts and puts the pressure on her to "work through" these feelings, rather than demanding that those creating toxic environments be held accountable.

Think about the language you use to refer to yourself. Instead of pathologizing your behavior and referring to your feelings as imposter syndrome, think of ways to empower yourself when you are feeling doubtful. Remember that you can build confidence and skill with practice, perseverance, and consistency.

Commit to giving yourself grace in unfamiliar situations, but also remember that in the situations where you have the skills and abilities, lean into confidence rather than doubt.

Embrace your worth and know that you belong in the spaces you inhabit. You were put there for a reason.

I stopped calling my doubt imposter syndrome. I acknowledge that there is trauma associated with not having been accepted or valued in some of the predominantly white spaces I have navigated. Rather than recall that trauma, I affirm within myself that I belong where I am and anything I need to learn to be more proficient can be accomplished. Until then, I am enough.

In reframing my relationship with the identification of imposter syndrome, I had to do some real soul-searching. After all, I had relied on that definition for why I felt the anxiety, nervousness, and doubt in the spaces I navigated for so long. So, I needed to unpack what those feelings really meant and where they were coming from in order for a meaningful paradigm shift in my thinking to take place. I started with the questions on the next page.

reflection questions

1. What is imposter syndrome?

2. When did you first feel that you experienced imposter syndrome?

3. How would you describe these feelings?

4. Where did these feelings originate from?

5. What happened in the interaction where you felt like you had imposter syndrome?

6. Where did this interaction take place?

7. What was said?

8. How did you react?

9. How did you feel prior to this interaction?

10. Did you feel like an imposter or were you treated like an imposter?

positive affirmations ───────────────

1. I am not an imposter.

2. I do not have imposter syndrome.

3. I have been treated like an imposter in the past, but that treatment does not define me.

4. I belong in every space I inhabit.

5. I deserve to be in any space I choose.

6. I do not allow others to define my worthiness when I enter a space.

7. My education, experience, and expertise are not framed by the perception of others.

8. Any doubt I have about my ability can be overcome with knowledge.

9. My value and knowledge are priceless.

10. I bring value to every space I inhabit.

In taking the time to carefully answer the questions, I thought about my own upbringing and how, like the typical "sufferers" of imposter syndrome, I did come from a family background that encouraged excellence. Yet, in the predominantly Black environments I grew up in, I never once felt like an imposter or doubted who I was. There were times when I felt like an outsider, like when I first immigrated to America. But never for one moment did I doubt my abilities to succeed and excel in any space I entered. That all changed when I stepped onto campus at the University of Florida. From the very beginning, I not only felt like an outsider, but also had my academic success and performance challenged and questioned daily.

Once I had answered these questions, I decided that I needed to put in the internal work to overcome this persistent perception that I had latched onto for most of my life. I had always bought into the idea that I was "afflicted" with imposter syndrome and needed to fix myself. When I reviewed the answers to my questions and really thought about each interaction where I felt that self-doubt, it became clear that I didn't have imposter syndrome at all. Rather, I had been reacting rationally to negative treatment, where I was being told, both implicitly and explicitly, that I was an imposter. And I knew without a shadow of a doubt that was not the case at all.

So, I began to repeat the affirmations to combat any creeping feelings of doubt that I had previously attributed to imposter syndrome. Part of eliminating any feelings of doubt is also embracing and leaning into the value of our authentic selves. If we are trying hard to assimilate and don't think that our true selves are valued, it becomes so much easier to fall back on the idea that we don't belong or are not good enough to inhabit predominantly white spaces. Being confident in our glorious selves, without hiding our authenticity, plays a big role in eliminating the negative and false narrative created by embracing the philosophy of imposter syndrome as a part of our reality.

Another area that we need to delve into in deconstructing feelings of self-doubt is to lean into the reasons why we feel this doubt and why we often are encouraged to or feel compelled to assimilate in our language, tone, speech patterns, and behavior when we enter predominantly white spaces. Part of learning not to embrace the idea that we are imposters is also to become 100 percent comfortable and confident with who we are. Authenticity is our superpower!

A big contributor to this feeling of being labeled as an imposter is the pervasive, harmful, and toxic narrative that says we don't belong. If we buy into that narrative by acting in a way that says our natural self is not good enough, we are reinforcing the notion that we are an imposter. By the very nature of the definition, an imposter is a pretender; an imposter puts on side. If I code-switch, change my manner of speaking, adapt my tone, and assimilate to an environment because I feel that who I am is not good enough, I have announced to my subconscious mind that I am an imposter. To combat that self-defeating loop, not only must we stop thinking of ourselves as imposters, we must also reject outward behaviors that perpetuate that idea within our minds.

code-switching and other exhausting behavior

"I was learning how to make myself
more digestible. I wasn't being
my most authentic self."

—Amanda Steinberg

For most of my professional career, I had been performing code-switching and other exhausting behaviors in white spaces. There were two catalysts that stopped me from perpetuating these behaviors. The first was a conversation with my podcast cohost at the beginning of 2020.

I was new to networking on LinkedIn and met a couple of guys who had just started a podcast on higher education. Both were white-presenting males, one of Puerto Rican descent and the other of Italian origins. Both came from the admissions, marketing, and administrative side of higher education. They asked if I would be interested in joining them as a guest host on their show. I gladly accepted. After the first interview, they offered me a permanent position, which I also accepted with gusto. As the cohost on that show, I recorded over three hundred episodes in almost two years. It was a worthwhile opportunity: I conversed with college and university leaders on an already-established podcast; in addition, I offered a unique viewpoint thanks to my specialized experience, not only as a faculty member, but also as an advocate for historically excluded and first-generation students. My experience in the edtech space became particularly helpful once the pandemic began and there was a pivot to online learning.

In 2020, we interviewed college and university presidents across the country about their plans, how they were accommodating students and addressing the digital divide, and on a variety of other topics. We spoke with high-profile leaders from colleges like Spelman, the University of Florida, Howard University, and more than a hundred others. It was exciting to be considered a thought leader in my field. However, there was a part of me that still felt a sense of trepidation every time I logged on to our Zoom calls to interview another university leader.

One evening, I was chatting about the show on the phone with one of my cohosts. Right before we hung up, he hesitantly shared something he had observed. He described how at ease and comfortable I was in our phone conversations, how easily I laughed, and how genuine and authentic I appeared in our interactions.

He contrasted it with how very reserved and tentative I acted with guests, as though I was afraid of saying the wrong thing; I didn't laugh or appear at ease; I was always serious. He never explicitly said he wanted me to speak the way I did with him. He just said, "I wish you were with them the way you are with me."

Even after that conversation, I still didn't change. Code-switching for me was putting on business attire to go into the office at nine o'clock. In my mind, it was a necessary evil that was part and parcel of being a professional. The global pandemic would later show us that was not necessarily the case; many of us started working from home on our laptops in pajamas, steps away from our bedrooms. But at the time, I still felt as though fully leaning into my natural and authentic voice would be a dealbreaker when speaking to people I admired and who were leaders in my field. I didn't want them to think I was unprofessional, so continuing my practice of adopting a voice and tone that I felt was more appropriate for an interview and where I wanted to be taken seriously seemed to be the most appropriate course of action at the time. After all, I had been doing that my entire professional career without a doubt that I was doing the right thing!

Witnessing the murder of George Floyd, shortly after that conversation with my podcast cohost, changed all of that. In fact, it flipped everything I thought about how I presented myself upside down. I'll never forget the moment I saw the murder on a major television broadcast. I had managed to avoid it all week with full knowledge that I would be traumatized if I did. And traumatized I was indeed—by the viral images of a Black man who could have been my brother, my cousin, or any of the men I grew up with. He was brutally and slowly murdered in front of my eyes.

I was triggered by the helplessness and hopelessness I felt when I watched his death and the subsequent outcry, not only around the country but across the globe. I also immediately felt struck by the revelation that, despite the common narratives, no matter what you do, you can still be a victim of trauma and even murder by people who perceive you as a threat. And this can simply happen because of how you look and sound and, more specifically, because you don't look—or sound—like them. There were so many narratives on both mainstream media and social media around the idea that George Floyd was a "bad" person. These narratives persisted until the murder conviction of the police officer, Derek Chauvin, just over a year later. Up until that time, the pervasive rhetoric was that George Floyd deserved to die because he had a criminal past. Some pointed to his history as someone struggling with drug addiction. Others insisted he brought this murder on himself by breaking the law and passing a counterfeit twenty dollar bill, whether knowingly or unknowingly. There were those who believed that if he had just complied with the police requests, then none of it would have happened. Deep inside, the majority of Black folk and many in the majority knew that wasn't true. And that's why the outcry about the injustice of what we all began to realize had been a public lynching was so widespread, loud, and insistent in the months after George Floyd was killed.

In addition, I began to think about my own false arrest and put it in context with the analysis and rhetoric about social justice and police brutality. One thing became clear: No matter how inconsequential my outcome had been in comparison to a man losing his life, I had been "doing the right thing." I was a college student, enrolled at a university within walking distance of where I had been arrested. I had been compliant and polite before, during, and after my false arrest, even though it took an unbelievable amount of restraint. In watching the media coverage, I was repulsed again and again by the idea that someone resisting arrest deserved to be killed—instead of being restrained in those circumstances. I remembered the first questions my mother asked me when she picked me up from jail: how had I been able to remain calm? And had I been tempted to run from the police? She was incredulous that I had been able to maintain my composure when I knew I was being arrested on false pretenses. I admitted that I had been incredibly tempted to run and, probably, might have even tried if I hadn't been able to calm myself down at that moment. The fight or flight reflex in humans is incredibly strong, and even stopping myself from yelling was extremely challenging. But I knew what would happen if I did.

Then, to add insult to injury, I had a receipt for the item I was accused of stealing with me the whole time. But I was still arrested, handcuffed, taken to jail, booked with mugshots, and fingerprinted. None of my compliance and "good behavior," which I'd hoped might evoke some type of sympathy or lead to redemption, had stopped an injustice from happening to me. It began to become crystal clear to me that my attitude toward the safety and security I was seeking by assimilating, toning myself down, trying to be "one of the good ones," and code-switching to be more acceptable, was entirely flawed. The narrative I had grasped onto since stepping onto the University of Florida's campus, that Black people can somehow control how we are treated by "behaving" and speaking "properly," disintegrated before my eyes. Someone could be lifeless on the ground and still be a victim of a society that refused to see the humanity in his Blackness. It was at that moment that I decided I would never look at my Blackness as a liability. My natural way of speaking, acting, and carrying myself would not be a source of shame or something to try to hide so I could assimilate more readily and seamlessly into predominantly white spaces. Rather, I decided to double down on my authentic self.

That meant that, from the time I made that decision, I never code-switched again. Whether I was speaking to a college president or a friend I went to high school with, my language, diction, tone, and volume of speaking stayed the same. My mannerisms remained the same. My laughter, which was frequent and raucous in every social situation I stepped into, stayed the same. I refused to moderate my authenticity in any way, shape, or form. And rather than repel people from me, as I thought it would, I found more opportunities were attracted to me than ever before in my life. All because of that one decision.

Code-switching is defined as switching from the linguistic system of one language or dialect to that of another.[61] In the Black community, most of us learn to code-switch between what we typically call African American Vernacular English (AAVE) and standard English at a very young age. We typically develop the skill when we first start attending school. And we're usually encouraged to do so by teachers, members of our community, and parents. It's seen as an essential skill for survival and success. Children growing up in African American communities, who natively speak AAVE, acquire a kind of bilingualism (or bidialectism) when entering mainstream American classrooms. Teachers and academic expectations they encounter require them to use standard, higher-prestige linguistic features for school assignments and classroom participation, often effectively leading these students to develop an ability to code-switch rapidly between nonstandard AAVE and standard English features.[62]

But the phenomenon of this duality in communication and mannerisms is not something new. It was first identified in WEB DuBois's *The Souls of Black Folk* in 1903. He describes it as a "sense of always looking at oneself through the eyes of others, of measuring one's soul by the tape of a world that looks on in amused contempt and pity.

"One ever feels his two-ness—an American, a Negro; two souls, two thoughts, two unreconciled strivings; two warring ideals in one dark body, whose dogged strength alone keeps it from being torn asunder. The history of the American Negro is the history of this strife—this longing to attain self-conscious manhood, to merge his double self into a better and truer self."[63] He continues, "In this merging he wishes neither of the older selves to be lost. He does not wish to

---

61   Merriam-Webster, 2022

62   Terry, J.M., R. Hendrick, E. Evangelou, and R.L. Smith. "Variable Dialect Switching among African American Children: Inferences about Working Memory." *Lingua* 120, no. 10 (October 2010): 2463–75. doi.org/10.1016/j.lingua.2010.04.013.

63   DuBois, 1903

Africanize America, for America has too much to teach the world and Africa. He wouldn't bleach his Negro blood in a flood of white Americanism, for he knows that Negro blood has a message for the world. He simply wishes to make it possible for a man to be both a Negro and an American without being cursed and spit upon by his fellows, without having the doors of opportunity closed roughly in his face."[64]

This explanation, from the sociologist, scholar, philosopher, writer, and first Black man to earn a doctoral degree from Harvard University, explains exactly why Black people tend to float seamlessly between using AAVE with friends and family, then using very traditional and often flawless English when we enter predominantly white spaces. We have been told from a very young age that the manner of speaking we are so comfortable with in those spaces won't be accepted when we're at school, on a college campus, in an interview, or at work. Comedian Dave Chapelle[65] famously joked that all Black people are bilingual because we use street vernacular and "job interview." We are taught from early on that speaking as we do "on the street," in our homes, at the cookout, or in our churches is not appropriate when we enter spaces where most of the people don't look like us.

And it doesn't stop at changing the language we use, the tone, and the loudness of our voices. We learn that there are other behaviors that are expected in white spaces. We may also change our mannerisms to be more acceptable. For many of us who grew up in predominantly Black neighborhoods, exaggerated hand gestures, shoulder shrugs, head movements, and anything else to express being animated when speaking are the norm. Growing up in South Florida, it was normal to see us standing around in a group speaking loudly, with our hands flying around us. From the outside, to someone not familiar with cultural cues, it might appear as if we were arguing. But that was just our way. We were like actors on stage, exaggerating and emphasizing every syllable we spoke.

---

64   DuBois, 1903

65   Chapelle, Dave. Interview by James Lipton. *Inside the Actor's Studio*, February 12, 2006.

But in spaces where the majority did not look like us, we were cautioned that those wild gestures would appear intimidating. Rather than be seen as endearing and funny, they might be interpreted as aggressive. I learned to temper them in college, ensuring that I was seen as more acceptable to my professors and classmates. I didn't laugh or speak too loudly either, another habit most of my friends and I had grown up with. Often whoever was the loudest was the one who got to finish their point or was applauded. That wasn't the case in the spaces I inhabited where I was the only brown face. Being loud and laughing raucously was met with quizzical looks of confusion. Eyes shifted away rather than being drawn to yours in admiration or shared amusement. We quickly learned to mute our voices if we didn't want to see those looks of disdain.

Once I entered the workplace, I learned that success meant not only knowing certain survival skills, but also becoming well-versed in them. It referenced what all our parents told us growing up. They had already explained that we would have to work twice as hard and be twice as good to be respected and to be successful in those spaces. As such, I adopted many behaviors that I later began to see were common among other Black professionals, especially the Black women I spoke to during my career journey.

I always wanted to be perceived as a dedicated worker, not a slacker. I didn't want anyone to say the Black girl was "lazy." To that end, I would typically arrive early for the workday and stay late. Even if I didn't stay extremely late, I always made sure I wasn't the first person to leave at the end of the workday. I would also exhibit other behaviors that I thought created the perception that I was a diligent worker. Often, I worked through lunch, grabbing something to eat at my desk to show how industrious I was and how dedicated to my job. I watched my coworkers go out to lunch together, often taking much longer than the allotted hour; I didn't do that for fear that people would think I didn't take my job seriously.

I was measured in my interactions, not only with my white coworkers but also with my Black colleagues. With white coworkers, I didn't speak up too assertively in meetings or challenge opinions, even when I knew I had something valuable to add. I tended to spend more time listening than adding to the conversations around me. When it came to my Black coworkers, I ensured I didn't spend too much time laughing and talking with them. After all, we didn't want to give anyone the wrong impression! Visits to their cubicles were kept short in the office, and the conversation was restricted to work-related talk, not what we did over the weekend, or the latest television show we were watching, or music we might both listen to.

According to *Harvard Business Review*,[66] code-switching is one of the key dilemmas that Black employees face around race at work. While it is frequently seen as crucial for professional advancement, code-switching often comes at a high psychological cost. For me, it led to extreme emotional, and even physical, exhaustion. Sadly, I didn't even realize how exhausting it was until I stopped doing it and felt an immediate shift in my energy. All the weight of creating a more palatable and acceptable alternate persona that truly wasn't my full authentic self was lifted. And it felt great! Researchers observed that seeking to avoid stereotypes is tiring work and can deplete cognitive resources and hinder performance. Feigning commonality with coworkers also reduces authentic self-expression and contributes to burnout.

Chief people officer of Grav Madison Butler[67] explains why code-switching is so harmful and destructive to the psyches of Black people in the workplace. "Societal traumas weigh on us like paperweights on origami birds, and we are

---

66   McCluney, Courtney, Kathrina Robotham, Serenity Lee, Richard Smith, and Myles Durkee. "The Costs of Code-Switching." *Harvard Business Review*, November 15, 2019. hbr. org/2019/11/the-costs-of-codeswitching.

67   Butler, Madison. "Code-Switching: We Are Never Getting Back Together." *Rolling Stone*, August 9, 2022. www.rollingstone.com/culture-council/articles/code-switching-we-never-getting-back-together-1393314.

expected to continue quietly, unbothered and unphased. From a young age, that is exactly what I did. I straightened my hair until the ends burned off, I changed my voice, and I only shopped in stores I saw my white classmates shopping in—anything to chameleon into their inner circles. I was unaware that I couldn't wash the Blackness off me—I could only disguise it. [...] I spent my teenage and early adult years running from myself because I felt that I was my own enemy in a world where success is painted in brushstrokes of white. I spent years hating myself because I believed that I inherently was my own enemy."

"Showing up wholly as yourself is not without risk," she continued. Regardless of the trend of employers asking people to 'bring their whole selves' to work, we haven't solved for the traumatic experiences that come with honoring our humanity at work. One study found 80 percent of Black women have felt as if they needed to change their hairstyle in order to be acceptable at work. We are conditioned to believe that the hair that grows out of our heads is not enough. [...] Oftentimes, employers ask us for authenticity without fully understanding that authenticity isn't painting our identities in happy colors but painting them truthfully. Authenticity is about the human experience. And let me tell you: The human experience is messy."

I made the decision to stop code-switching at the beginning of the pandemic. We had recently started sheltering in place; the country was experiencing an awakening about what it meant to be Black in America; and most of us were navigating the challenges that came with working from home. Deciding to stop the behavior I had identified as exhausting and traumatic wasn't as hard as I initially thought it would be. We were already jumping on Zoom calls for meetings in sweatpants after rolling out of bed the hour before. We had seen our coworkers' children running through the background or watched their cats walking on their computer keyboards. It didn't seem that far-fetched for me to ditch my assimilated Valley-girl accent and very precise manner of speaking to slide into using AAVE with my down-South drawl as I did when I talked to my family and friends. So that's where I started. And no one batted an eyelid.

I would get on Zoom calls and just speak in my natural and authentic way. I wasn't measured. I wasn't calculated. I just spoke "normally" as I would in any other interaction.

And I had another revelation. There wasn't anything "unprofessional" about how I was speaking. I was just being myself.

The only difference was that I was no longer prioritizing what I had previously determined was the comfort of everyone else. I had always thought that, to succeed, I had to hide my obvious Blackness because of the negative connotations associated with it; I was to assimilate more closely to those that didn't look like me. And of course, I couldn't hide the color of my skin. So, the logical option was to speak and act like those in the majority.

In their surveys of approximately three hundred Black college-educated employees in the United States, researchers for *Harvard Business Review*[68] found that Black people downplayed their race (e.g., "I try not to act like other members of my racial group"), avoided stereotypes (e.g., "I avoid behaviors that would make people at work think that I am lazy"), and promoted shared interests with majority-group members (e.g., "I try to talk about topics that other people would find interesting") through adjusting their behavior and appearance. Once I decided adjusting my manner of speaking, tone of voice, and loudness were actions I was no longer willing to take, it became clear that the other exhausting adjustments to my personality, habits, and appearance would have to stop too.

I reasoned that if pearl stud earrings were professional, then so were gold hoops. If a soft pink lipstick was professional, a bright pink lipstick was equally appropriate. I no longer engaged in the mental gymnastics required to be sure I was acceptable to those that didn't look like me. My only goal was to maintain my professionalism while being true to myself in every interaction, both in

---

68   McCluney et al., "The Costs of Code-Switching."

i'm not yelling

person and on Zoom call meetings. I had the transformative realization that I needed to choose my authentic self and emotional well-being over the comfort of those in the majority in the spaces I inhabited. And I never looked back after I made that choice.

Initially, there were people who discouraged me from being "too" authentic. The backlash started when, shortly after George Floyd was murdered, I started posting so voraciously on social media. In one interaction, an older "well-meaning" white man in his sixties explained that he thought I was being irresponsible to advise Black people not to code-switch. He further reasoned that workplaces are places of business, professional spaces, and aren't like a basketball court where people can talk trash and curse.

I paused for a moment to evaluate his statement, then asked him one question: "Why do you perceive that Black people speaking authentically involves them talking trash and cursing?"

He paused as well to reflect on my question. "I'm not sure why I said that," he said after a moment. "I'm sorry."

But that is precisely the issue. The onus is placed on Black people to speak, act, behave, and dress in a manner that mimics those in the majority. But there really isn't a clear reason why, other than the fact that who we are in our natural, authentic state is seen as undesirable—not worthy of being in those spaces. And sadly, research has concluded—just as I had when reflecting on my arrest—that, no matter what we do, our behavior and efforts to assimilate, conform, and behave in a way that we perceive as more acceptable in and of itself is not the answer we are looking for to create the opportunities we deserve. Even if it does open doors because we are deemed more "professional" or "acceptable," what is the ultimate cost to our mental and emotional well-being?

It was unclear whether code-switching enables Black employees to be accepted as "professionals" in the workplace. To answer this question, *Harvard Business Review*[69] designed an online experimental study of almost 350 Black and white participants recruited on CloudResearch and living in the US to determine how they evaluated code-switching behaviors.

The participants were instructed to imagine themselves as recently hired employees at a law firm in a large city. They each read an email from a colleague named either Lamar Matthew Jackson or La'Keisha Renee Jackson, both third-year associates at the firm. In the email, Lamar or La'Keisha shared advice on the "unspoken" ways to succeed at the company: whether you should "be yourself" or try to fit in; use standard English or slang; or wear your hair "naturally" or conform to more traditionally "Eurocentric" hairstyles. Participants were randomly assigned to two conditions in which Lamar/La'Keisha code-switched by altering their preferred name (e.g., "My name is Lamar/La'Keisha, but you can call me Matt/Renee at work"), speech patterns, or preferred hairstyle depending on workplace expectations.

Participants then evaluated whether Lamar/La'Keisha's behavior was appropriate for the workplace and level of professionalism. On average, white participants evaluated code-switching behaviors positively and perceived those who engaged in these behaviors as more professional—particularly when Black employees adjusted their hairstyle to better fit the norms of the dominant group. "You should be allowed to keep your name, but slang and nappy hair are unprofessional for the workplace," said one respondent. Another noted, "Looking and behaving professionally are necessary when working at a place like that. Appearances matter. Her name La'Keisha sounds obviously 'Black' and some may even think 'ghetto,' but Renee is more conservative."

---

69   McCluney et al., "The Costs of Code-Switching."

Ultimately, I decided it wasn't worth it. I found that the more I leaned into my authentic way of expressing myself, my natural mannerisms, and even the way I dress with gold hoop earrings, bright colors, and bold lipstick, the more people liked me, Black and white alike. I went from cohosting a podcast on higher education to becoming the host of my own podcast on the Ebony Covering Black America Podcast Network, where I interviewed almost two hundred Black leaders across every industry. I had at least a dozen opportunities to speak for corporate organizations around the country. I even had one of my social media followers donate $25,000 so that I could start a scholarship fund for young Black women at Spelman College. He's the CEO of a huge multimillion-dollar tech company, who started engaging with my content very early in my journey of speaking out so transparently. One of the first things he said to me was that he was inspired by how I showed up, speaking my truth without reservation. In each of those instances when the opportunities were offered, the interaction started with the reason the support was being offered. And it was always because they were so impressed with how authentic I was.

Given my own experience and based on the studies and research, my advice to Black women is to be yourself! Don't allow anyone to create a narrative that perpetuates a myth that your authentic, genuine, and whole self is not good enough for a space you inhabit. From the moment you wake up in the morning until you sit at the head of the boardroom table, empower yourself to walk in your truth. I made a conscious decision to stop code-switching, and it dramatically improved my emotional well-being and the quality of my life. I became more confident and self-assured. I never questioned whether I had made the right decision because, as soon as I made it, a world of opportunity opened up for me. But I encourage anyone attempting to determine what authenticity and showing up as themselves looks like, and whether they can successfully navigate that transition in the places they inhabit, to answer these questions.

reflection questions

1. What actions do you consider code-switching? If you've determined that you are code-switching, answer the following questions:

2. Do I code-switch in my day-to-day activities, and if so, how often?

3. When or where does this behavior occur?

4. How long has this behavior been occurring, and when did it first start?

5. What do I perceive are the benefits of code-switching?

6. How do people react when I code-switch?

7. How do I feel when I code-switch?

8. What would be involved with discontinuing this behavior?

9. How would I feel if I stopped code-switching?

10. What would be the benefits of not code-switching?

positive affirmations ————————————

1. I am more than enough.

2. My authentic self is my real self.

3. My authentic self is valued in every space that I inhabit.

4. My authenticity is a gift.

5. Being myself is my superpower.

6. I will shine brighter than ever in my truth.

7. I step into my power using my authentic voice.

8. Everything about my voice speaks to the power of truth.

9. My truth is valuable.

10. My whole self is a precious jewel.

To step into the true power of our authentic voices, we must uncover the true richness, tone, cadence, intonation, pacing, and language of that voice. If we are constantly code-switching and hiding the authenticity of that voice, we will never tap into its greatness. If we're always modifying and altering what that voice sounds like to accommodate the comfort of those who don't look like us, we will never be able to harness the power of our voice. If we are imitating the voices of those in the majority, rather than leaning into the collective of voices that have been ours for generations, we are leaving a lot of our true potential unheard. That's why it's imperative that we focus on nurturing and embracing what we have inside us and letting that shine in all its amazing glory.

We need to embrace our true selves in more than just the way we speak or our mannerisms. It's also about loving the beautiful, natural appearance of our bodies, skin, and hair. When we step into the true power of our authentic voices, another part of that power is harnessing the narrative of what our appearance means and determining how we have internalized that story. Black women's voices have often been shamed as being too loud and aggressive. But the same is often said of our appearance.

Maybe it's natural hair in an afro, locs, or braids. Perhaps it's a bold lipstick or brightly colored makeup. But our hair has often been the biggest point of contention because, unlike the other aspects of our physical appearance, it's not easily changed without chemical processes or artificial enhancement. The natural hair that grows out of our bodies has been politicized and often shunned as being unkempt or radical in appearance. Many of us were taught at a young age to not only control our tongues, but also control our tresses. But this is yet another exhausting and never-ending cycle of behavior that tells us we don't belong, so we develop imposter syndrome. It stands to reason that, if we're being taught and internalizing the narrative that the way we speak as well as the way we appear is inappropriate for professional spaces, we would question whether we belong in those places at all. Being able to stand in the total truth of who we are in every aspect is essential to our continued growth, development, and success in any endeavor we pursue.

chapter 5

afros, locs, twists, and braids—the politics of natural hair

"I am not my hair."

—India Arie

I'll never forget the first time I wore my afro out for a job interview. It was the first time I remember feeling self-conscious about my hair. This was long before I had thought deeply about the implications of my natural hair during my tenure working in the online learning space. But several years in, being a faculty member was starting to wear on me. I knew I had so many other gifts and skills to offer to the right organization.

I had scheduled the job interview for a sales trainer position with a cutting-edge educational technology company that provided software and support to many of the large distance-learning universities I had worked for. And even though I didn't have the specific skill sets they were looking for, I knew my transferable skills were on target. I had spent quite a few years working in the online learning space. I was also a classroom teacher with a great deal of experience in face-to-face instruction of adult nontraditional learners. In addition, I had almost a decade working in sales, primarily in the online recruiting space. I had also served in a senior capacity as a trainer for my team. I reasoned that I had a pretty decent shot at nailing the interview and getting the job. Granted, I hadn't run a sales department. But I had worked for some of the power players in the industry that this organization pitched products to, so I decided to give it a shot. After I submitted my resume for the opening, the email from the recruiter to set up the interview confirmed my confidence in potentially getting hired for the position.

The morning of the interview, I had a crucial decision to make. Would I be wearing my natural hair out in its normal state, which at that time was a chin-length afro? Or should I wear it pulled back in a more conservative bun? Mental gymnastics controlled my mind as I quickly got dressed, applied makeup, and grabbed breakfast on the morning of my interview. Staring in the mirror, I grabbed my curls and pulled them back from my face in a tight bun at the nape of my neck. Alternatively, I let my coils plop into a fluffy halo around my head. I reasoned that the company was cutting-edge in the tech space and was known for innovation. People working in this space are known to be more open-minded, creative, and esoteric in their thinking. And sales tends to be a more personality-

i'm not yelling

driven department, with many people showing their fun and quirky sides when interacting with potential clients and building the rapport needed to close a deal. The afro would show my fun and out-of-the-box sense of style. The afro it was! I fluffed it out and headed to my interview.

I arrived early and introduced myself to the receptionist. She promptly requested I take a seat and advised they would be with me shortly. But something about the energy seemed off. The receptionist wasn't friendly. In fact, she seemed to look at me with disdain. I shook it off: maybe she was having a bad day, I reasoned. She spoke briefly to a woman who appeared to be the person I would be interviewing with. The woman glanced over at me disinterestedly and quickly walked past where I was sitting in the lobby without even making eye contact. She walked past me several more times as I waited at least thirty minutes past my interview time.

Exasperated, I wondered if I should just get up and leave. But I had already waited so long. I decided to just wait patiently. This was a very exciting opportunity, and I didn't want my impatience to sabotage an interview I knew could open a whole new world in my career. The interviewer finally walked through the lobby once more, this time approaching me and introducing herself. She never apologized for the extended wait. Instead, she advised me to follow her, since the team was waiting for me. I was stunned but tried to pull it together, masking my feelings by putting a broad confident smile on my face. First, the long wait time. Then, the news that this would be a group interview. But as a college professor, I felt able to pull a group presentation together quite quickly. And that would be the case, as she gave me the topic to present on as soon as we walked through the doors. I entered a small meeting room with about a half-dozen men and women sitting around a small table. They were all laughing and talking as I walked in.

I strutted into the room and flashed a wide smile. I gave everyone a warm hello, with some lukewarm responses from the group. As I walked into the room, I noticed there were poster boards stuck on all the walls. I could tell they were there from the previous interview candidates. The large group of people seemed tired and distracted. As a college professor, I can always tell when I have the attention of an audience and they are engaged. They were not engaged at all. In fact, they appeared bored, no matter how dynamic my presentation was. I started to question my decision to wear my afro. Because this was a sales position with a cutting-edge edtech company, I hadn't second-guessed myself up until that point. Did they think my afro was too sassy? Did I appear unprofessional? I was inside my head during the latter part of my presentation and could feel my energy and enthusiasm drifting downhill. I finished up the presentation, hastily gathered my belongings, and left after the interview. Of course, I didn't even receive a follow-up email to say that they had decided to move forward with the other candidate. But I hadn't expected them to send me a courtesy note either.

I remember feeling slightly dejected as I drove home, thinking about their smug faces and the fact that they had left me waiting in the lobby for more than thirty minutes. The lack of consideration they had shown me was infuriating. They didn't even have the courtesy to take down the poster boards from the previous presentations! But I also realized they had done me a favor. While I couldn't say for sure if their lukewarm response to me in the interview had anything to do with my vibrant afro, I did know one thing: I never wanted to feel doubt or lack of self-worth because of how I chose to wear my hair in a professional setting. Because of my afro, I'd felt self-conscious, doubting I was good enough—and I'd let it affect my performance. Never again. That was a turning point, and I wore my afro and natural hairstyles in every job interview after that incident. If someone doesn't want me in a space because of my hair, then I don't want them. And they're probably doing me a favor by rejecting me early in the process, so I don't have to endure a toxic or unsupportive work environment. The truth is, I would never know unless they blatantly said something directly about my hair. But regardless of the fact, I made a commitment to accept the beauty of my own natural hair, no matter what I perceived others would think.

Once I embraced my natural hair fully, I did experience more incidents of more blatant "othering" about my appearance. There were times when I would walk into an office and coworkers would express surprise, make bewildered expressions, or be overly effusive when they saw my afro puffed out in a joyous halo around my head. On more than one occasion, colleagues attempted to touch my hair without asking or only asking when their hands were already tentatively touching my coils with wonderment in their expressions. I often had white people express surprise when I switched from braids to a blowout to an afro puff all within the timeframe of a couple weeks. This was as though hair extensions were something that was unique to Black women when we all know they're not. And forget about wearing a wig! I often went from short natural hair to a long flowing wig with color highlights, as a protective style. Sometimes I did this on a weekly basis. It was always sure to elicit surprised, unsolicited, and unprofessional responses as soon as I sat down at my cubicle in the morning.

But being "othered" because of our hair is nothing new to Black women in America. The origins of hair discrimination have deep roots, beginning when African women first set foot on American soil. Diasporic Africans in the Americas have experimented with ways to style their hair since their arrival in the Western Hemisphere well before the nineteenth century. During the approximately four hundred years of the trans-Atlantic slave trade, which extracted over twenty million people from West and Central Africa, their beauty ideals have undergone numerous changes.

Africans captured as slaves no longer had the hair-grooming resources that had been available to them in the motherland. The enslaved Africans adapted as best they could under the circumstances, finding sheep-fleece carding tools particularly useful for detangling their hair. They suffered from scalp diseases and infestations due to their living conditions. Enslaved people used varying remedies for disinfecting and cleansing their scalps. For example, they applied kerosene or cornmeal directly on the scalp with a cloth as they carefully parted the hair. Enslaved field hands often shaved their hair and wore hats to protect their scalps from the sun. House slaves had to appear tidy and well-groomed. The men sometimes wore wigs mimicking their masters', or similar hairstyles, while the women typically plaited or braided their hair. During the nineteenth century, hair styling, especially among women, became more popular. Cooking grease, such as lard, butter, and goose grease, was used to moisturize the hair. Women sometimes used hot butter knives to curl their hair.[70]

Because of the then-prevalent notion that straight hair (which, unlike kinky hair, is common in people of European origin) was more acceptable than kinky hair, many Black people began exploring solutions for straightening, or relaxing, their tresses. One post-slavery method was a mixture of lye, egg, and potato, which burned the scalp upon contact.

In the eighteenth century, tignon laws in Louisiana were even enacted. These laws forced Black women to cover their hair with scarves to distinguish their status as either free or enslaved. The Code Noir, or Black code, was a French law that restricted the lives of people of color living in French colonies. Originally created in 1685 for the Caribbean colonies, it was extended to Louisiana in 1724. Spanish authorities enacted similar laws in 1769 and 1778.[71]

By 1786, Esteban Rodríguez Miró was the Spanish governor of Louisiana. He disliked actions some Black women had taken, considering them to show "too

---

70   Hargro, Brina. "Hair Matters: African American Women and the Natural Hair Aesthetic." *Art and Design Theses*, August 11, 2011. doi.org/10.57709/2102391.

71   Christovich, Mary Louise, Robin Derbes, and Roulhac Toledano. *New Orleans Architecture: Faubourg Tremé and the Bayou Road*. Pelican Publishing Company, 2003.

much luxury in their bearing."[72] White women began to urge Miró to act to restrict the fashion of non-whites.[73]

The tignon law (also known as the chignon law) was a 1786 law that forced Black women to wear a tignon headscarf. It was in part intended to halt the practice of plaçage unions by which ethnic European men entered civil unions with non-Europeans of African, Native American, and mixed-race descent. Its intent was also to tie freed Black women to those who were enslaved.[74]

Virginia Gould writes that the true purpose of the law was to control women "who had become too light skinned or who dressed too elegantly, or who, in reality, competed too freely with white women for status and thus threatened the social order."[75]

Looking at this fact from a historical perspective gave me even more insight into the discomfort projected onto me by white women whenever I navigated predominantly white workspaces. White women always seemed to be the ones feigning surprise that I could have my hair in braids one week and have a teeny-weeny afro the next. They were typically overly effusive with their compliments about my bodacious hairstyles, as though my ability to transform myself radically from week to week made them uncomfortable. Understanding that this wasn't happening in one moment in time, just to me, but was a historical pattern of Black women being shamed about our hair, gave me perspective.

---

72   Johnson, Jessica Marie. *Wicked Flesh: Black Women, Intimacy, and Freedom in the Atlantic World*. University of Pennsylvania Press, Incorporated, 2020.

73   Kein, Sybil. *Creole: The History and Legacy of Louisiana's Free People of Color*. Louisiana State University Press, 2000.

74   Clinton, Catherine, Michele Gillespie, and Inc Netlibrary. *The Devil's Lane: Sex and Race in the Early South*. New York: Oxford University Press, 1997.

75   Kein, *Creole: The History and Legacy*.

Solita C. Roberts,[76] image coach and consultant, emphasizes the importance of Black women embracing the mindset shift necessary to step into their authenticity in their personal style, professional wardrobe, hair, and makeup. This can even extend to how Black women dress to conform to arbitrary workplace norms. "It's every Black woman saying I will show up as my authentic self—natural hair, bold colors, red lipstick, and take my place in leadership. As Caroline Wanga said, 'Who you are is nonnegotiable.' I believe when women redefine the beauty standard of how they should look, what they should wear, and how they should show up, we change the narrative on issues like ageism, appearance bias, and discrimination. We change the single story of women in the world simply by being who we are. [...] Carnival has been my thing and I love the colors, the energy that they give me. So, I pull that part of my personal love and infuse that into my personal style. So, when I'm working, you know these women, it's like, 'Okay. What are some things that you like? What are some personal parts of you?' And as simple as, 'I wish I could wear my natural hair! I don't think I can wear my natural hair.' "[77]

She tells about one time when a colleague asked her how the boss felt about her natural hair. "And I was like, 'I don't understand. What do you mean? Do you mean this thing that's growing out of my head? What do you mean about that?' Because I'm that person who will ask you the question, so you can repeat your answer and be sure that that's actually what you're asking me. Because I'm not going to assume that you meant something else. Let's clarify. Let's get down to the meat of what you mean. You mean this that's growing out of my head. It's like me acting dumb, but making sure that you realize what you asked me is stupid." She continues, "So, we go through that process of removing those limiting beliefs, removing those outside voices that are telling you [that] you

76   Roberts, Solita C. "I Think Fashion Is Sexy!" *LinkedIn* (blog), September 2022. www. linkedin.com/posts/solitacroberts_linkedintopvoices-fashion-imagecoach-activity-6973618335674482688-SgZ7?.

77   Leiba, Elizabeth, and Solita C. Roberts. "Unaired Episode." Produced by the Ebony Podcast Network. *Black Power Moves*.

can't do this or you can't wear this or you can't show up that way. Then we craft your personal style. What does *that* look like?"[78]

Rather than concluding that white women and others in the majority found my hair distasteful or unprofessional when I entered workspaces, I started looking at the historical evidence that they found it intimidating. Based on the history of their interactions with Black women's hair, white women had typically been jealous and envious of our hair. That was why they tried so hard to control it, "other" it, and insinuate that we should assimilate our hair to look like theirs to be accepted. This knowledge created a level of acceptance of my beautiful coils that I had never had before! My glorious, puffy halo wasn't anything to be ashamed of. People's reaction to it, particularly white women, wasn't my concern. My goal was to walk in the radiance of my natural hair that grows out of my scalp. But our psychological journey of getting to a place of comfort in that beauty has been a long and winding one that continues even today.

After the American Civil War and emancipation, many Black people migrated to larger towns or cities, where they were influenced by new styles. Some continued to wear their natural hair. Others straightened their hair to conform to white beauty ideals. They wanted to succeed and to avoid mistreatment, including legal and social discrimination. Some women, and a smaller number of men, lightened their hair with household bleach. A variety of caustic products that contained bleaches, including laundry bleach, designed to be applied to afro-textured hair, were developed in the late nineteenth and early twentieth centuries, as Black folk demanded more fashion options. They used creams and lotions, combined with hot irons, to straighten their hair.

The Black hair care industry was initially dominated by white-owned businesses. In the late nineteenth century, Black women entrepreneurs such as Annie Turnbo Malone, Madam C. J. Walker, Madam Gold S. M. Young, and Sara Spencer

---

78   Roberts, "Black Power Moves."

Washington revolutionized hair care by inventing and marketing chemical (and heat-based) applications to alter the natural tightly curled texture. They rapidly became successful and dominated the Black hair care market.

Scholars debate whether hair-straightening practices arose out of Black desires to conform to a Eurocentric standard of beauty, or as part of their individual experiments with fashions and changing styles. Some believe that slaves and later Black people absorbed prejudices of the European slaveholders and colonizers, who considered most slaves second-class, as they were not citizens. Ayana Byrd and Lori Tharp say that they believe the preference for Eurocentric ideas of beauty still pervades the Western world.[79]

In the United States, the successes of the Civil Rights Movement, and the Black power and Black pride movements of the 1960s and 1970s, inspired Black folk to express their political commitments by adopting more traditionally African styles. The afro hairstyle developed as an affirmation of Black African heritage, expressed by the phrase, "Black is beautiful." Angela Davis wore her afro as a political statement and started a movement toward natural hair.

But the popularity of natural hair has waxed and waned. In the early twenty-first century, a significant percentage of Black women still straightened their hair with relaxers of some kind (either heat- or chemical-based). This is done even though prolonged application of such chemicals (or heat) can result in overprocessing, breakage, and thinning of the hair. Rooks[80] argues that hair care products designed to straighten hair, which have been marketed by white-owned companies in Black publications since the 1830s, represent unrealistic and unattainable standards of beauty.

---

79   Byrd, Ayana D., and Lori L. Tharps. *Hair Story: Untangling the Roots of Black Hair in America*. New York: St. Martin's Griffin, 2001.

80   Rooks, Noliwe M. *Hair Raising Beauty, Culture, and African American Women*. New Brunswick, NJ: Rutgers University Press, 2000.

Sales of relaxers took a steep fall among African American women from 2010 to 2015. Many Black women gave up relaxers to go back to their natural roots. Research has shown that relaxer sales dropped from $206 million in 2008 to $156 million in 2013. Meanwhile, sales of products for styling natural hair continued to rise. But this rise in the popularity of Black women finally embracing their natural hair texture once and for all has exposed the historical trend of discrimination in predominantly white spaces, particularly in the workplace. Increasing research suggests Black women with natural hairstyles, such as curly afros, braids, or twists, are often perceived as less professional than Black women with straightened hair. This is especially true in industries where norms dictate a more conservative appearance.

The findings, published in the journal *Social Psychological and Personality Science*,[81] offer empirical evidence that societal bias against natural Black hairstyles infiltrates the workplace and perpetuates race discrimination. This is according to Ashleigh Shelby Rosette, a management professor and a senior associate dean who conducted the research at Duke University's Fuqua School of Business.

The impact of a woman's hairstyle may seem minute, Rosette said, "but for Black women, it's a serious consideration and may contribute to the lack of representation for Blacks in some organizational settings. In the aftermath of the George Floyd murder and the corresponding protests, many organizations have rightly focused on tactics to help eradicate racism at systemic and structural levels. But our individually held biases often precede the type of racist practices that become embedded and normalized within organizations."

To detect bias against Black women with natural hair, the researchers recruited participants of different races and asked them to assume the role of recruiters screening job candidates. Participants were given profiles of Black and white

---

81   Koval, Christy Zhou, and Ashleigh Shelby Rosette. "The Natural Hair Bias in Job Recruitment." *Social Psychological and Personality Science* 12, no. 5 (August 19, 2020): 194855062093793. doi.org/10.1177/1948550620937937.

female job candidates and asked to rate them on professionalism, competence, and other factors. Black women with natural hairstyles received lower scores on professionalism and competence and were not recommended as frequently for interviews compared with three other types of candidates: Black women with straightened hair and white women with curly or straight hair, the researchers found.[82]

The CROWN Coalition was founded in early 2019 with the goal of expanding legal protections against discrimination for people of color who choose to wear their natural hair. With the help of a diverse array of organizations in the social justice, business, legal, and education sectors, the coalition's alliance of organizations, including founding members Dove, National Urban League, Color of Change, and the Western Center on Law and Poverty, are working to create a more equitable and inclusive experience for Black people through the advancement of anti-hair-discrimination legislation, known as the CROWN Act.

One of the women I met in the past year, who is determined to champion the rights of Black women to wear their natural hair without fear, is Adjoa B. Asamoah, one of the cofounders of the CROWN Coalition. She is very clear about her mission, her passion, and her "why" to champion a movement ensuring Black women don't receive backlash in the workplace. Unfortunately, so many women are being discriminated against every day, with Black women one and a half times more likely to be sent home from work because of their hair.[83]

82 Duke University Fuqua School of Business. "Research Suggests Bias against Natural Hair Limits Job Opportunities for Black Women." Duke Fuqua, August 12, 2020. www.fuqua. duke.edu/duke-fuqua-insights/ashleigh-rosette-research-suggests-bias-against-natural-hair-limits-job.

83 Dove-US. "The 2021 CROWN Research Study for Girls." Hair Discrimination Research: Dove CROWN Studies, 2021. www.dove.com/us/en/stories/about-dove/hair-discrimination-research.html.

In our conversation,[84] Asamoah was resolute in the ultimate goal of pushing this legislation forward. "The CROWN Movement is about outlawing race-based hair discrimination, which is different than just hair discrimination. A lot of people don't really know what [it] is, although we are certainly working to ensure that more people truly understand what it is and what it is not. It is acknowledging our racial identity; fully recognizing that there is no biological basis for race the way we use it. But that doesn't mean that *racism* is not very real. [...] It is truly about outlawing race-based hair discrimination, which has been problematic for so many reasons, not just creating school environments that are not conducive to our babies thriving, not just enforcing and reinforcing these Eurocentric standards that have been an excuse to Black folks be passed over for promotions or have offers of employment rescinded."

She further explains, "You're talking about a racial wealth gap that exists for so many specific reasons, and then you're going to add to that based off of my hair; the way my hair grows out of my head or my decision to wear a protective style that's consistent with my [racial] identity. That has been fulfilling work, but it has also been very eye-opening. There have been cases where this bill has passed overwhelmingly. Champions, like our former Assemblywoman Tremaine Wright in New York, who passed the bill first; in California with former Senator Holly Mitchell, who introduced the bill first, it has been passed in those two states overwhelmingly. [...] Then you see some states that won't even put the bill on the agenda to be heard or to be read. A bill like the CROWN Act essentially doesn't cost anybody anything to just leave me and my hair alone, not making it to the agenda in certain states. So, all that means is we have to push forward. We obviously have a lot of work to continue, but we have been here before. We are cut out to do it. It does not mean that we are not exhausted. We have to remember that rest is part of the movement as well. Then we get up, and we push forward."

---

84   Asamoah, Adjoa B. "Championing the CROWN Act." Interview by Elizabeth Leiba. *Black Power Moves, EBONY Covering Black America Podcast Network,* February 7, 2022. ebonypodcastnetwork.com/black-power-moves.

The CROWN Act, which stands for "Create a Respectful and Open World for Natural Hair," was introduced to clarify that traits historically associated with race, such as hair texture and hairstyle, should be protected in the Fair Employment and Housing Act (FEHA), including in the workplace and in K–12 public and charter schools.[85] The CROWN Act passed recently along party lines with a vote of 235–189 and now heads to the Senate for a vote. Several states have already implemented their own versions of the CROWN Act. Massachusetts became the latest state to pass a local ban on hair discrimination.

"Hair discrimination is rooted in systemic racism, and its purpose is to preserve white spaces," the NAACP says.[86] "Policies that prohibit natural hairstyles, like afros, braids, bantu knots, and locs, have been used to justify the removal of Black children from classrooms, and Black adults from their employment." The discrimination Black women have always faced due to the appearance, texture, and perceptions of our natural hair strikes at the heart of the matter regarding its politicization and the power struggle that ensues.

Hair discrimination starts from the time we are very young. According to the latest CROWN Research Study for Girls, 53 percent of Black mothers whose daughters have encountered hair discrimination, say that their daughters have experienced race-based hair discrimination as early as five years old. The study also demonstrates that 66 percent of Black children in majority-white schools have faced race-based hair discrimination—and 86 percent of those children have experienced it by the age of twelve.[87]

---

85   National Urban League. "Ending Hair Discrimination in the Workplace with Dove and the CROWN Coalition." Nul.org, 2022. nul.org/news/ending-hair-discrimination-workplace-dove-and-crown-coalition.

86   NAACP. "Natural Hair Discrimination FAQ." Legal Defense Fund, n.d. www.naacpldf.org/natural-hair-discrimination/#:~:text=Hair%20discrimination%20is%20rooted%20in.

87   Dove-US, "The 2021 CROWN Research Study."

The report reveals that 100 percent of Black elementary school girls in majority-white schools (who report experiencing hair discrimination) experienced discrimination by the age of ten. And despite 90 percent of Black children stating that their hair is beautiful, 81 percent of Black children in majority-white schools say they sometimes wish their hair was straight.[88]

Based on these experiences, from a young age we have been taught to fear our natural hair and everything that it represents. We have been told a narrative that has been passed down from generation to generation. Then we begin to have experiences that reinforce those stories. Those negative ideas are then repeated and perpetuated in mainstream media images and the interactions we have with those in the majority; we come to believe that wearing our natural hair is a threat to the status quo. Not assimilating through making our hair conform to the aesthetics dictated by those who do not look like us is regarded as problematic. Not covering it or declining to straighten it chemically or with heat, is seen as an act of rebellion. We're conditioned to believe that that stance would only be taken by those who have no concern about their place in the hierarchy of society.

The only acceptable and professional alternative, as well as the only option, was to abandon the natural hair of our childhood as soon as we were old enough to start relaxing it to meet those standards. Although we have seen waves of resistance to this narrative, the rise of internet access to information on how to transition to natural hair, with what has been called "the big chop," began to open Black women's eyes up to the beauty of natural hair, how to take care of it, products and styles that were available, as well as online communities of support. This led many Black women to abandon this negative narrative to proudly embrace the natural hair that grows out of our scalps no matter the consequences.

---

88   Dove-US, "The 2021 CROWN Research Study."

Published in 2016, the article entitled, "African American Personal Presentation: Psychology of Hair and Self Perception,"[89] gave the rundown on an experimental procedure conducted in America, using data from five urban areas across the country and females ages eighteen to sixty-five. A questionnaire was administered which determined how "African American women internalize beauty and wearing of hair through examination of locus of control and self-esteem." The results showed a positive correlation between high internal locus of control and wearing hair in its natural state. American women have a feeling of empowerment when it comes to sporting their natural hair.

As Black women who choose to wear our hair in its unprocessed state as it grows out of our scalps, we must embrace the fact that our hair is not a liability. In fact, as the CROWN Act makes its way from the House of Representatives to the Senate, there is hope for federal legislation to ban racial hair discrimination. And it is already illegal to discriminate against natural hair in at least fourteen states. In embracing our natural hair and our journey to acceptance of it, it's critical for us to keep in mind there's no right or wrong way for us to embrace our hair if we are being authentic and true to our own wants, needs, and desires. Just as with code-switching, where there are degrees to which someone may or may not code-switch based on where they grew up, the environments they navigated and who they typically socialize with, the same can be said of the natural hair journey. Some Black women keep their hair unprocessed at all times. Some press it or blow-dry it to make it more manageable. Some women wear wigs and weaves. Other women love to wear braids. Styles aren't as important as the freedom to choose, even if it's a relaxer, provided that it is based on our own desires rather than feeling forced to conform, feeling "othered," or feeling a need to fit in to be accepted.

---

89   Ellis-Hervey, Nina, Ashley Doss, DeShae Davis, Robert Nicks, and Perla Araiza. "African American Personal Presentation: Psychology of Hair and Self Perception." *Journal of Black Studies* 47, no. 8 (July 27, 2016): 869–82. doi.org/10.1177/0021934716653350.

Any place that would discriminate or make you feel uncomfortable because of your natural hair or cultural hairstyles is not a place that is safe or nurturing for your emotional well-being. So, it's more important that we embrace our own hair, our own natural state of being, and our own comfort. This extends to our feeling safe and accepted in the spaces we inhabit. Having confidence in the appearance of our hair and knowing that it's not unprofessional or a hindrance to our ability to be successful is an invaluable part of maintaining the awareness and attitude that we belong in every space we inhabit. We don't have to change anything about our physical appearance that is an inherent part of our identities and who we are as Black women—unless we want to and on our own terms. Changing our hair should be a choice based on the day of the week and our mood. It is not a strategy to be more acceptable and to assimilate in predominantly white spaces, particularly the workplace.

My hair is a crown and I wear it proudly! Those who are troubled by it are troubled by me as a whole. And deciding to be your whole self in every way is empowering. It creates a mind shift where, instead of seeking permission to be in a place, feeling tentative or unsure, you walk into that space owning it in every respect. You know that you are more than worthy to inhabit it in the entirety of your personhood, from the top of your head to the soles of your feet. That level of self-acceptance is very significant for Black women, who've been told that our appearances are not as appealing and haven't consistently had our images affirmed. I found that by intentionally doing it for myself, what I saw in mainstream media, magazines, and social media became secondary to what I saw in the mirror. I affirm myself every day to remind myself that natural hair in all its glory is my crown, and it adorns my head as the queen that I am.

reflection questions

1. What are your earliest memories about your natural hair?

2. Do you remember the first time you were aware of your hair and its relationship to your overall identity and appearance?

3. How did these memories inform your relationship with and attitude toward your hair?

4. Do you feel you developed a positive or negative relationship with your natural hair? Why or why not?

5. Were you aware of the statistics from the CROWN Research Study for Girls? What are your thoughts regarding those statistics? Did they align with any of your own childhood experiences?

6. If your hair was ever chemically processed, when did you first begin to relax or chemically straighten your hair?

7. What was the process of straightening your hair like, and how did it evolve over time?

8. If you wear your hair naturally, what made you make the decision? What has your experience been since that time? How do you feel about your natural hair?

9. Have you experienced discrimination in the workplace or "othering" in predominantly white spaces based on your natural hair?

10. Are you aware of the protections offered by the CROWN Act? Has it passed in your state? How will that knowledge affect your navigating professional spaces with your natural hair?

positive affirmations ——————————————

1. My natural hair is my crown!

2. My natural hair is beautiful.

3. My natural hair is professional.

4. My natural hair is unique in all its various forms and styles.

5. The way I wear the hair that grows from my head is entirely up to me.

6. No one can touch my hair without my explicit consent.

7. My hair reflects my mood, not my competence or professionalism.

8. Natural hair *is* professional.

9. I do not provide explanations about my natural hair.

10. My natural hair is my choice, and I have the freedom to make that choice.

Navigating spaces and learning to deal with some of the affronts to our authentic selves, such as our natural way of speaking, wearing our hair, and being is a part of empowering ourselves in places that were not designed with us in mind. Speaking up is a key strategy. But also deciding when spaces are not welcoming, and determining whether we should stay in them, will be an ongoing consideration.

chapter 6

i'm not yelling—the psychology of micro-aggressions

"If you are silent about your pain,
they'll kill you and say you enjoyed it."

—Zora Neale Hurston

A couple of years ago, when my organization went through a buyout, there was one new member of the team that acquired our institution who would constantly interrupt and speak over me on areas of my expertise, even though he wasn't knowledgeable about them. At first, I wondered if I was being too sensitive. After all, this was a tense time in my career. After working diligently, leading projects, and demonstrating my expertise in project management in the C-suite of my institution, I had earned two promotions. We were now being acquired in the middle of a global pandemic. A series of management meetings took place to determine the direction of the organization after the merger.

The organization that bought us was relying on many of us in the leadership team to offer insights so they could determine a strategy to create the much-needed synergy to drive the new institution forward. As such, my insight was often called on in those initial strategy meetings, as someone who had worked in the corporate office for six years. But what I kept finding was that my insights would be challenged by some of the more junior members of the transition team, who all happened to be white men and women. They would challenge points I brought up for consideration and even outright reject the answers to questions they had just asked me in our team Zoom meetings!

I remember feeling so frustrated by the back and forth in one meeting that I sighed out loud, looking up to the ceiling to gain my composure. And at one point I was so tired of being interrupted that I stopped the offender and asked him to let me finish my point before he interjected again. There was an awkward silence on the Zoom call as all the faces on tiles on my laptop stared at me in disbelief. I felt a moment of discomfort, but also satisfaction. How was it fair that I was the only one being placed in a situation where I felt uncomfortable? If invoking a feeling of discomfort was what it took to stop this behavior in the future, then I was willing to endure it. I'd had enough!

My immediate supervisor at the time called me after the meeting and advised that I was not to be so outspoken in those types of situations. She cautioned that my being verbal or even displaying nonverbal signs that the behavior was bothersome would place an unwanted target on my back. "You need to learn to fix your face!" she warned me.

I was disappointed by her scolding. "It sounds like you're more concerned with my behavior than with the person who won't stop talking over me and interrupting me," I countered. "I'm the victim in this situation and, rather than address his behavior, you're talking to me!"

My frustration with her lack of empathy was at a boiling point. I felt my heart racing, as my voice rose, and I began talking faster. Hearing the lack of recognition about why I was so upset led to my ending the conversation abruptly. I had always respected her as a leader. As a Black woman, she had worked her way up to the position of vice president within the organization. And as a Black woman, I thought she would be more understanding. But she wasn't. Not at all. Her primary goal was to maintain the status quo as we moved through the process of merging our respective departments. Within a few months, she had left the organization and taken a leadership role elsewhere.

That conversation really brought home the mistaken perception that it is up to those who are on the receiving end of microaggressions to be sure that the perpetrator of this type of behavior and those witnessing it, who are not preventing it, are made comfortable. In any other professional setting, inappropriate or unprofessional behavior is acknowledged, discouraged, and corrected. This applies to anything from rudeness, excessive tardiness and absenteeism, lack of attention to detail or adherence to deadlines, inaccurate communication, and overall poor job performance, to higher-level illegal actions like sexual harassment. And the corrective actions will certainly come from managers with Performance Improvement Plans all the way up to termination.

In cases of racial microaggressions, there is a veil of silence surrounding the sharing of discomfort with managers. This is especially evident for those of us with managers who are white. We witness the actions taking place and no one is batting an eyelid. We've been interrupted and spoken over several times, even when we've been asked a question or are the subject matter expert. We are often asked multiple times to quantify why we're qualified to even weigh in on or answer the exact same question we've been asked! Sometimes we suggest ideas or strategies only to have them ignored or dismissed. But when the same action plan comes from a white male, it's embraced and lauded.

We look at it as the cost of doing business. We chalk it up to the Black tax that our parents told us we'd have to pay. We remind ourselves that we already knew we'd have to work twice as hard. After all, isn't that what our parents, teachers, mentors, and everyone else told us growing up in our communities? So, we put our heads down and ignore what's happening to us daily. We smile with sullen eyes, knowing that all around us what has happened didn't even register in the consciousness of the white faces we're surrounded by. They are oblivious to our pain. It's an emotional trauma that caused the tears as we pulled into parking lots of office buildings long before the global Covid-19 pandemic relegated most professionals who had previously been in offices to working from home. And it was the reason for the deep breaths and quick sighs before we walked into a meeting or conference room. During the pandemic the same occurred, but it was right before we turned on our webcams to face our coworkers and bosses for those "essential" weekly check-in Zoom meetings. But at least working from home brought us some reprieve from these toxic behaviors and environments we had previously had to tolerate in person.

And these behaviors are dismissed as a figment of the victim's imagination. They are discounted as not serious, and the person on the receiving end is perceived as being "too sensitive" or, even worse, as a "troublemaker." In addition, it's something that most of us know will only bring more attention to us and often create the negative attention we fear will cause us to be targeted, overlooked for promotions, and seen as too emotional or unprofessional for pointing out the negative behavior, which stops us from even addressing it in the moment or bringing it up later with mentors or supervisors in any attempt to be proactive in stopping it.

Regardless of my manager's reservations, I noticed that my coworker didn't continue to interrupt me in future meetings. It was scary to point out inappropriate behavior but also necessary at that moment, because I was tired of it. No matter how scary or awkward it felt, I knew that if I didn't say something, there was no chance whatsoever that it would stop. And as the corporate restructuring continued, I experienced the same phenomenon again and again from other white managers, both men and women. What was most troubling was not just how often their inappropriate behavior occurred, but also how tone-deaf and often offensive their comments were and how blissfully unaware they were of the inappropriateness of their behavior and, by extension, the harm they were causing.

There were a few lessons learned from this experience. First, I had never really been exposed to collaborating with higher-level corporate leaders who were white. I saw that they often refused to acknowledge expertise, knowledge, or suggestions from me or from another member of my team, who was also a Black woman. The fact that both of us were most knowledgeable about the operations of the corporate office after being with the organization for two decades between the two of us, with four master's degrees and a doctorate degree between the two of us, they still constantly questioned our suggestions and offered up their own strategies, then threw literal tantrums during meetings when we "gently" tried to explain why they wouldn't work. Witnessing some of these dynamics was eye-opening for me as someone who'd had only minimal exposure to predominantly white corporate leadership. But one thing it did was teach me to be more vocal. I had always been taught, and had learned from watching others, that the safest way to survive in these predominantly white corporate spaces was to attract the least amount of attention possible. But I found that survival strategy in an environment where I had assumed a leadership role central to the success of my department. My position opened me up to more opportunities to receive microaggressions, less opportunities to be quiet because of the necessity for my leadership, and more need to be vocal, if only to protect my own emotional and mental well-being.

That sounds great in theory, but for Black people navigating predominantly white spaces, sometimes there is a fear of asserting ourselves and correcting microaggressions. This is because we're not exactly sure what they are. We know that there are times in our daily interactions with coworkers or managers when we become uncomfortable. But we can't pinpoint what makes us feel that lack of ease. Sometimes we shake it off because we can't identify what made us feel triggered in that moment.

Another characteristic of microaggressions is that they are often framed as though they are compliments. Therefore, the offender projects the ultimate gaslighting experience by feigning ignorance when we correct their behavior or if we are justifiably offended.

Solita C. Roberts, image consultant, recounts[90] an incident that occurred when she interviewed for jobs as a recent immigrant. "I immigrated from Antigua to the US in 2019. I was bright-eyed and bushy-tailed as to what my new life is going to look like, and I remember being in an interview. This gentleman asked me, 'Do you speak English?' I was like, 'Am I not in an interview? Am I not speaking English?' I started to second-guess myself. I don't want interviews where, because you hear I'm an immigrant, [you] automatically assume that English is not my first language or for some reason I'm not qualified for the job of answering your phone."

---

90   Roberts, "Black Power Moves."

Kanika Tolver, author and CEO of Career Rehab, adds[91] that for Black women these types of microaggressions can be particularly traumatic. "Me being a Black woman in tech and being the only Black person on the team, or the only female, I have dealt with my own workplace trauma. I've shared that some of the things I hear is that [Black women] feel like people are not respecting them. [...] Even in remote work, [Black women] are feeling like there's those same microaggressions that they dealt with in the office. They are still taking place through email, through Zoom, through Skype, through WebEx. Whatever these technology tools that we all have been using, they feel like people don't have true accountability with their managers. They feel like their managers are saying one thing in private and doing another thing in public to them. There's no true allyship. We have fake allyship."

"Black women always feel like we're not being heard," she explains. "It's causing [Black women] to have anxiety, depression, stress. It's affecting their physical state of mind, the spiritual state of mind, their emotional state of mind, and causing them to have nervous breakdowns. I can attest to being one that has experienced all three of those things because of being in a toxic work environment. We need to focus on how to navigate those challenges and then how to heal from those challenges. [...] A lot of times Black women have been so focused on navigation that we have not been focused on healing. And the fact that we haven't healed from past bad career relationships [means] we're taking that same baggage, that same drama, and those same low expectations into the new career relationships."[92]

She adds, "What we're finding is that we do that in our personal lives. We may go from this man to that man, and we may take that same baggage with us. I really think that a lot of us have trauma that has nothing to do with the job, and

91   Tolver, Kanika. "Rebuilding Your Personal Brand and Rethinking the Way You Work."
      Interview by Elizabeth Leiba. *Black Power Moves. EBONY Covering Black America
      Podcast Network,* January 27, 2022. ebonypodcastnetwork.com/black-power-moves.

92   Tolver, "Rebuilding Your Personal Brand."

i'm not yelling

we haven't even unpacked that trauma. When we're doing this, we're bringing some of that with us. We're colliding our personal trauma, our career trauma, and I always say a lot of times our career isn't right because our life isn't right. We haven't dealt with the things from our past, so how can we have the expectations of someone to love and care for us when we don't even love and care for ourselves outside of corporate? [...] We're giving to everyone else. We're giving to our families, our kids, our parents, our significant others. I think we need to stop even expecting people to understand. We have to say enough is enough. I'm going to seek professional help."

A recent issue of *Perspectives on Psychological Science*[93] focused exclusively on the topic of microaggressions. This issue contained a systematic review of 138 studies documenting and categorizing them, describing their harmful effects, and identifying coping strategies.

The review found clear evidence that daily experiences of racial microaggressions harm the psychological and physical well-being of minorities. Data indicate that racial microaggressions are linked to low self-esteem, increased stress levels, anxiety, depression, and suicidal thoughts. People of color who experience microaggressions are more likely to feel sadness, anger, and hopelessness. Other studies have found that people who experience microaggressions are more likely to report stomachaches, headaches, sleep disturbances, and high blood pressure. Other research has demonstrated people who encounter regular microaggressions are more prone to use alcohol and tobacco.[94]

---

93 Association for Psychological Science. "Current Understandings of Microaggressions: Impacts on Individuals and Society." *Association for Psychological Science - APS*, September 13, 2021. www.psychologicalscience.org/news/releases/2021-sept-microaggressions.html.

94 Fagan, Abigail. "The Detrimental Effects of Microaggressions." *Psychology Today*. October 5, 2021. www.psychologytoday.com/us/blog/evidence-based-living/202110/the-detrimental-effects-microaggressions.

A recent study by the Harvard Business Review found that open racism and sexism are astonishingly omnipresent in today's workplaces: 81 percent of women of color in tech said they experienced at least some racism, while 90 percent reported the same for sexism.[95] Understanding that women across the board are subject to both blatant and more subtle racism, in spaces that should be deemed safe and professional, takes the onus off of us to parse through what is acceptable and what is not. Someone thinking you are the receptionist when you're the director of the department, someone saying you're "so articulate," someone asking about your background to quantify your ability to weigh in on a conversation—all these behaviors constitute microaggressions and create an unbelievable mental and emotional toll that adds up over time.

Given that microaggressions are so emotionally, and even physically, harmful and that their perpetuation thrives in an environment where they are ignored, victims are gaslighted. To gaslight someone means to manipulate another person into doubting their own perceptions, experiences, or understanding of events, according to the American Psychological Association. And many Black women experience being persuaded into believing they are being "overly sensitive" or imagining affronts, and the behaviors often remain unacknowledged, both by those committing them and by leadership in corporate spaces. The key to maintaining healthy energy and minimizing the effects of gaslighting is to first acknowledge that they are a thing. As a collective, Black people, and particularly Black women, affected by them are not playing a big hoax on corporate America. We are not pretending our workplaces are rampant with this toxic behavior. So, reminding ourselves that it's not just us is critical to maintaining control in a situation that otherwise seems out of control.

_____

95   Williams, Joan C., Olivia Andrews, and Mikayla Boginsky. "Why Many Women of Color Don't Want to Return to the Office." *Harvard Business Review*, May 12, 2022. hbr. org/2022/05/why-many-women-of-color-dont-want-to-return-to-the-office.

Having a working definition of what a microaggression is helps us to frame the behavior. As a result, we can process our own feelings about what happened and then address it in the moment if we choose to take that approach. So, what is a microaggression? That's the thing. We know what it is when we experience it, but a formal definition is a bit trickier.

When I was interviewed by Dana Brownlee, senior writer for *Forbes*, for her article "Microaggressions Are Often Misunderstood. Here Are 5 Dangerous Myths to Be Aware Of," we discussed this challenge. Many of us have some degree of confusion about exactly what constitutes a microaggression. And another element that makes them a challenge to define is the regularity with which they occur and the variety of types of behavior we encounter in predominantly white workplaces daily.

I found the Webster's Dictionary definition insufficient because it didn't adequately reflect my experiences as I saw them: "A comment or action that subtly and often unconsciously or unintentionally expresses a prejudiced attitude toward a member of a marginalized group (such as a racial minority)."

By categorizing microaggressions as subtle, unconscious, or unintentional, it minimizes the responsibility of the person committing the act as well as the amount of harm inflicted. Even the name "microaggression" gives the impression that it's no big deal or something that can be overlooked. Nothing could be further from the truth. In that same article, the experiences of Black women in corporate spaces illustrate just how pervasive and elusive they are.

Although "micro" leads one to believe they're small, the impact can be significant—often described as death by a thousand paper cuts. "Simply put, microaggressions are deflating," explains co-director of Cultural Diversity and Inclusion at Power Home Remodeling, Olumide Cole.[96] "Not only do they negatively impact individual employees, but they also impact the work and business overall. With each microaggressive comment or action, it becomes more emotionally exhausting and harder to bounce back. [...] Racial microaggressions include white employees assuming that a Black employee is of a lesser employment status, asking a Black coworker to get you a cup of coffee or copies, asking a Black woman if you can touch her hair, requesting a white supervisor because you think a Black supervisor 'isn't a good fit,' asking a Black employee how they got their job, commenting to a Black coworker that he is "so articulate," or referring to a Black employee as 'you people.' "

An example of a microaggression is expressing a belief that race doesn't make a difference in success in life. For example, "If you just work harder, you'll succeed." Another example is a white male saying, "I succeeded because I wasn't lazy and didn't rely on society to help me." The meaning behind these statements is, if I can succeed on my own, you can too—there is nothing stopping you. However, these statements don't consider the entitlement one experiences when they are white. It is simply easier to get hired if you are white, based entirely on your race—not your competence.[97]

Another distinction I pointed out during my conversation with Dana was that microaggressions are just as much about what is unsaid as what is said during these harmful and uncomfortable interactions.[98] Sometimes it isn't something verbal, like an insensitive comment or speaking over you. Often,

---

96   Brownlee, Dana. "Microaggressions Are Often Misunderstood. Here Are 5 Dangerous Myths to Be Aware Of." *Forbes*, December 6, 2020. www.forbes.com/sites/danabrownlee/2020/12/06/microaggressions-are-often-misunderstood-here-are-5-dangerous-myths-to-be-aware-of/?sh=a1d493e9bfa3.

97   Sarkis, Stephanie. "Let's Talk about Racial Microaggressions in the Workplace." *Forbes*, June 15, 2020. www.forbes.com/sites/stephaniesarkis/2020/06/15/lets-talk-about-racial-microaggressions-in-the-workplace/?sh=5a7f4bd25d28.

98   Brownlee, "Microaggressions Are Often Misunderstood."

it's ignoring your input or devaluing your contributions with a dismissive attitude, facial expression, or body language. All these small affronts add up until they often become virtually intolerable.

This explains exactly why so many Black professionals are hesitant, and even outright resistant, to return to the office after working from home during the Covid-19 pandemic. According to a recent study by Future Forum, a research firm developed by Slack Technologies, the workplace communication company, just 3 percent of Black professional workers were accepting of heading back into the office full time.[99] For two years, we experienced reduced exposure to toxic work environments; we got a reprieve from daily microaggressions, the pressure to code-switch and conform to dress codes that focus on assimilation, natural hair discrimination, and office politics. This has allowed us to thrive in what we do best, shining for our productivity and ability to do our jobs. While working from home, the emphasis hasn't been on what we look like or how we sound. We have been relatively insulated from environments where these daily affronts take a toll on our mental and emotional well-being. That reprieve has been welcomed and is not something most of us are willing to give up easily.

Finding a community of support was an important part of my being able to acknowledge when microaggressions were happening, not internalize the behavior or place the blame on myself, and develop the courage to address the harmful actions in the moment. I was lucky enough to develop a community that began with one coworker on my job, then expanded to Black women I met across the country by networking on LinkedIn. In the year after George Floyd was murdered, many of us posted about our experiences with these behaviors and found stunning similarities in what we had endured in these spaces, how we had been mistreated by coworkers and leadership alike, and

99   Subramanian, Sheela. "A New Era of Workplace Inclusion: Moving from Retrofit to Redesign." *Future Forum*, March 11, 2021. futureforum.com/2021/03/11/dismantling-the-office-moving-from-retrofit-to-redesign.

what our responses had been. And the lack of acknowledgement by those committing the microaggressions was par for the course. The gaslighting about what they were doing was standard as well. But as we all began to share our stories, a sense of empowerment, shared unity, and collective strength was developed.

One was a leader at the state level in education for her organization. She was implementing Social Emotional Learning programs in K–12 schools statewide. Yet subordinate staff on her team routinely participated minimally in her meetings and informed her that she was too expressive and intimidating. When she brought her concerns to her supervisor, she was told she needed to adjust her management style so they would feel more comfortable with her. She was told her staff feared her, and that it was her responsibility to fix it!

Another woman worked as a communications director for a top university. She recounted how doubts about her abilities, subtle attacks resulting in feelings of psychological unsafety, and toxic work environments culminated in suicidal ideations and a medical leave.

The chief people officer for a major organization and DEI advocate explained how she had been brought in and contracted by another organization to lead a workshop on anti-racism. Immediately, upon starting her presentation, one of the participants began to challenge her on the definitions of anti-racism language. She immediately had to defend her knowledge to deliver a presentation to a roomful of employees of an organization that had contracted her and paid her to train them.

The biggest lesson I learned in the years that I have been doing this advocacy work is that sharing our stories peels back that layer of shame that people who are doing inappropriate behavior count on. When they make us think we're to blame, we internalize what they've done and give them protection to keep doing it again and again. By asking others about their experiences and sharing our own, we are often confronted with the reality that is validated by numerous studies, research, and surveys. This reality is that most of us are enduring the exact same behavior, and we're suffering in silence! These same kinds of nurturing environments can be developed in professional organizations, employee resource groups, sororities, mom groups, or Facebook groups.

Speaking up demystifies microaggressions. Even if the definition itself seems complicated, abstract, or murky, if several of us have experienced the same action that made us feel uncomfortable, felt inappropriate, and caused us to question why it was even occurring, chances are that behavior needs to be addressed. Communities of support enable us to speak out not only to protect ourselves, but also to hold perpetrators accountable so that their actions can be prevented in the future.

One question Dana asked me in our discussion about microaggressions was whether I felt they should be addressed in the moment or if it was more tactful to wait until a later time. My suggestion is always to address an issue immediately after it occurs. As with all verbal communication, people tend to "forget" the details and nuances after the conversation is over. A few days later, I think it's a lot easier for someone to obscure what happened or try to convince you that you're remembering it wrong.

If a microaggression occurs verbally, my tactic is to stop the conversation at that moment. I will point out that what was said made me feel uncomfortable or that I felt it was inappropriate. I give the person the opportunity to acknowledge what they've done and create space for a teachable moment. And I've done that with coworkers and managers alike. Here's the thing about this type of behavior. The perpetrator is counting on us to be too uncomfortable, feel like we are responsible, and feel too awkward to call them out on their behavior. I revert back to my days of teaching in college classrooms. When inappropriate behavior occurs, the student is betting that they can get away with it because you won't want to stop the class, bring attention to the problem, and create an awkward flow in the classroom dynamic. That tactic always backfired in the classroom because I would do just that. But the power dynamic in a classroom is different. The professor is obviously in control of the power of the floor. The student disturbing that flow is trying to dismantle that power dynamic.

But the same does apply in a meeting, even if we're not in management within the organization. If we're conducting a meeting, during that time frame we are a leader, regardless of our title or place on the organizational chart. And if someone says something inappropriate, it's our responsibility to shut that behavior down immediately, just like I did in my classroom. I started to look at the power dynamic. I started to look at why Black women were deferring to people who were derailing their presentations, asking inappropriate questions, or making comments that were unnecessary. And it comes back to that power dynamic. Even though we are speaking, that person, just like an unruly student, is exhibiting passive-aggressive behavior to throw us off our game. My goal during those dynamics started to be to assert control in those situations just as though I was in my classroom. I didn't distinguish whether the person was a coworker or a manager. My only objective was to determine if they were doing or saying something that didn't add to the discussion at hand. And if it made me feel uncomfortable, I simply stated that and called it out for what it was: inappropriate.

I realize this may sound too simplistic, easier said than done, or even dangerous. And that's exactly what people in the majority want us to believe. My manager, a Black woman, was certainly not immune. She cautioned me about being too outspoken in defending myself against microaggressions. She warned that the target would be on my back. But in truth, the opposite was the case. Addressing the behavior stopped it from occurring at that moment. I felt more empowered to defend myself if it did happen again.

And it did create a sense of boundaries that had not been there before. By setting those boundaries, people know not to mess with you. It's the same principle I always applied to classroom management. Students will push your limits unless you clearly define them. And they must be nonnegotiable, just as they are in any other relationship. For some reason, at work, we lose a sense of what's acceptable or not, deferring to letting people have their way because we don't want to seem like troublemakers. That is abusive, toxic, and harmful to our mental health.

I'll admit the first couple of times were awkward. My first time correcting someone's behavior came on a conference call. A coworker who was leading a project I was overseeing, but was not my direct report, asked me why I was getting "so excited" about a plan to make some changes to our action plan. I remember looking over at my teammate in disbelief. We were both in the office speaking to this white woman on speakerphone. I wasn't excited at all. I was speaking at a normal volume and rate. I was speaking quite slowly because I was explaining an issue and determining some strategies we might be able to use to address the outcomes. I stopped the conversation at that moment and told her I didn't feel comfortable with her referring to my normal tone as "getting excited." There was an awkward silence. She broke it by admitting she was stressed out about the changes that needed to be made. I acknowledged that and moved on with the rest of the call.

After the meeting ended, I asked my teammate, another Black woman, if I had seemed "excited" or agitated as had been insinuated. She replied that I had been neither angry nor yelling. And this is why sometimes we don't speak up about microaggressions. We second-guess ourselves. We wonder if there is some merit to what the person is saying. We blame ourselves and wonder if perhaps we did do something wrong. But in such an intimate setting, it was easy to see that she was the problem and not me. She said she was stressed. She may have unintentionally perpetuated the stereotype of "the Angry Black Woman" in that moment. I wasn't sure of her intent. But that wasn't my concern. My concern at that moment was to make sure she was more careful in how she addressed me or any other Black women. She'd used harmful archetypes that are inappropriate regardless of her stress level about a deadline.

I remember feeling very anxious and dejected after that interaction. I questioned myself quite a bit, even after the affirmation from my coworker. I had always had a pleasant relationship with this woman. In fact, we had worked together at another organization previously. I replayed the scenario repeatedly in my head, wondering if there was something I had missed that could have caused her to react in that way. So that's where the guilt also comes into play. We have been victimized but, even then, wonder what we could have done differently to avert aggression against us. My teammate reassured me that I was not at fault. But still, it was hurtful. I knew I didn't deserve to be mistreated. And obviously, she realized what she had done was wrong as well because, by the end of the week, I had received an email where she apologized for her behavior.

That's what calling people out will do. It holds them accountable. Seeing that result encouraged me to continue addressing microaggressions whenever they happened. This was not just for me, but also for other Black people, and particularly Black women, that these individuals interacted with. If I didn't, they would think their behavior was okay. If they thought their behavior was okay, they would keep doing it. If they kept doing it, they would continue to create toxic and harmful environments for other Black folk and the cycle would continue. I decided to break it. I decided that if I had anything to do with it, it would stop with me. So, I faced it every single time.

Speaking up and out about microaggressions is just one more strategy we as Black women can use to continue to empower and embolden ourselves when we step into predominantly white spaces, particularly the workplace, with all its landmines. Being confident the toxic behavior we're encountering is not a figment of our imagination, or self-induced because of something we have done, is also healing to our own mental and emotional well-being. The gaslighting is real around microaggressions. As a result of being called out, and then having to acknowledge them, the perpetrator must examine their own behavior and change, both in the present and in the future. Most people are not ready to do that amount of self-reflection. But that's the only way for real change to happen. And whether they have the long-term motivation and drive is not necessarily your concern. They will need to determine their own capacity for self-development. But by speaking up, you are at least changing the dynamics of them expecting that their behavior will remain unchecked. Ultimately, there would be an expectation that this would improve the culture of your workplace over time. I did see it happen in my department. They learned that certain behaviors would not be tolerated because I was unrelenting in calling them out. Remember, your goal is to preserve your own well-being in that space at that moment and for as long as you inhabit it. Taking control of how you are treated in spaces that don't reflect you is a big part of that process.

reflection questions

1. What is a microaggression?

2. Have you ever experienced microaggressions in the workplace?

3. What has been your response to these types of workplace behaviors directed toward you?

4. How did these behaviors make you feel?

5. How did microaggressions affect your ability to navigate the professional spaces you have inhabited?

6. What are some strategies you might be able to utilize to address microaggressions when they occur?

7. How do you feel about some of these strategies and how effective might they be, given your specific workplace culture?

8. What communities of other Black women are available to provide support when you experience workplace-induced trauma from microaggressions?

9. Do you have coworkers or leaders within your organization with whom you can safely discuss your concerns if you experience microaggressions?

10. What strategies are you using to nurture your emotional and mental well-being?

positive affirmations

1. My voice belongs in every space I inhabit.

2. No one can silence my voice without my consent.

3. I address inappropriate behavior whenever it happens.

4. I protect my space and my peace.

5. Inappropriate behavior does not belong in any space I inhabit.

6. Inappropriate behavior directed toward me is not a reflection of me.

7. When asked to speak, I own the floor.

8. I will not allow myself to be ignored.

9. I am a subject matter expert and more than worthy of respect.

10. I demand respect in every space I inhabit.

The confidence to demand respect in every space we inhabit, and to correct any behavior that is not in alignment with that declaration, is crucial in our journeys to successfully navigate workplaces where most people do not look like us. Navigating these types of environments and not always having the correct advice or guidance about how to handle challenging situations always brings home the realization of how critical mentorship is in the workplace, especially from like-minded Black women.

opening the door— mentorship, sponsorship, and sisterhood

"A mentor is someone who allows you
to see the hope inside yourself."

—Oprah Winfrey

I've never had a mentor. At least, I have not had a mentor in the true sense of the word. My experience working in nonprofit spaces, in higher education, and then in social justice advocacy gave me a great deal of exposure to amazingly influential people. But I never really understood how to initiate and then cultivate a relationship that would lead to the guidance and support I knew could be experienced with mentorship.

Over the course of my time speaking with dozens of Black women whom I met on social media, one recurring theme came up. It was the importance of mentorship and how valuable it had been in their personal and professional development. Those women helped me to reframe my ideas about what mentorship is and what it needs to look like. They deepened my understanding of how to identify a suitable mentor, and how to develop and nurture that relationship in a way that feels authentic and mutually beneficial.

Stephanie Sylvestre, Harvard University Advanced Leadership Initiative fellow, has spent much of her professional life studying mentorship. She understands how influential having a mentor can be to personal and professional success. "I think that people can grow and develop if they have great mentors, and usually you start off life with the original mentors, your parents, who are guiding you and shaping you into the best human that you can possibly be. I think that people are also able to reach their full potential if they have help, and mentors are one of the many ways that you can get help. [...] I've just had lots of amazing things happen in my life because of mentors. One of my huge mentors, advocate, supporter self-selected to be my mentor about eighteen years ago. A lot of great accomplishments that I have been able to achieve [are] because of her being my mentor and helping me, and so I just believe that mentoring works. I have tangible data points, real world experience, and then of course there's tons of literature on the importance of mentorship. So that's the reason why I'm so passionate about mentorship."[100]

Christy Rutherford,[101] CEO of Vision International, is a sixteen-year Coast Guard veteran and the thirteenth Black woman to achieve the rank of Commander Lieutenant Colonel equivalent in the Coast Guard's 230-year history. She explains the importance of people being able to advocate for you in that sponsorship relationship. She also explains how to be intentional about seeking a mentor, as well as the concept of having multiple mentors, rather than only one. This is based on the various areas of your life where you might need guidance.

"Mentorship seems like this tough thing," she says. "I got a mentor, and then I got another mentor. So, by the end of my career, I had thirteen mentors... white men and Black men. Because before I make a decision, this is chess. I need somebody who's two levels above me. So that's my advice to women. You need somebody who's been where you are, and you need multiple people who are experts in their field. [...] So, every person that I call has a gift. One person worked in personnel. One person was a politician. One person was the pastor. I was like, 'You better pray for me!' So, I had different people who had different relationships that worked in different fields. And when something happened, I would call that person to give me advice on what I should do. So, a mentor—you should have at least three of them."

She explains, "What I didn't have was a woman mentor. I was prepared for my seat at the table as an officer and as a Black officer because a lot of my mentors were men. I wasn't prepared for being *the* Black woman. That's a whole different

---

100   Sylvestre, Stephanie. "Black Women and the Importance of Mentorship." Interview
       by Elizabeth Leiba. *Black Power Moves, EBONY Covering America Podcast Network*,
       January 13, 2022. ebonypodcastnetwork.com/black-power-moves.

101   Rutherford, Christy. "Helping Black Women Manifest Dream Careers." Interview by
       Elizabeth Leiba. *Black Power Moves, EBONY Covering Black America Podcast Network*,
       January 22, 2022. ebonypodcastnetwork.com/black-power-moves.

battle, because there is going to be one position that you get to where you need a woman because men and women process information differently. And the men couldn't help me process what was going on. But a part of me now being a mentor and a sponsor was I had so many battles that I fought. My gift is to serve. I'm going to turn around and make sure that women don't fall into the same hole."

Mentorship can come in many shapes and forms. But however it comes, it's comforting to know you have someone that you can rely on—someone who has your back. And preferably that is more than one woman that you can call on. And another key lesson is to look outside the preconceived notions of who a mentor should be. Mentorship doesn't necessarily need to be one person. And it's more effective if you have multiple mentors with a variety of skill sets and types of insights. These mentors are the ones you can call on when you have questions, need help, or want guidance. But for many women, this is where we get stuck. We're not sure exactly what we're looking for; we only know we'd like someone to talk to and to give us advice, whether within our organization or someone who is skilled in business or entrepreneurship in general. Since we're often the only, or one of the few, Black women within our organization, we're not sure how to approach or identify appropriate mentors; we're not even sure exactly what we need from them if we are able to develop that connection.

In delving into the benefits of mentorship, it became quickly apparent that statistically, professionals who had been most successful had engaged in some form of formal or informal mentoring relationship during their career. This correlation, backed by research, became clear from my conversations; it is also evidenced by most Black people reporting that they have not had any significant professional mentorship and guidance. I wanted to understand why, since it was clear that this would be a key to improving outcomes in the workplace.

According to a 2011 LinkedIn survey[102] of nearly a thousand women in the US, 82 percent agreed that having a mentor is critical to the trajectory of your career. And yet one in five women never had access to a mentor, with over half of those respondents reporting that they were never able to find someone appropriate. "Appropriate" is a qualifier that can be broad in its interpretation but is also heavy with meaning for women. And as with the gender pay gap, in which Black women make significantly less than their white female counterparts, Black women have a tougher time—in no small part because they see less representation in the leadership roles generally sought out for mentorship.

According to the Women in the Workplace report[103] published by McKinsey & Co. and LeanIn.org, job experiences are not improving for women of color. The 2021 report is based on data and insights from 423 companies representing over twelve million people and survey responses from over 65,000 individual employees. The representation for women of color in the C-suite was 4 percent, versus a whopping 62 percent for white men. It was 20 percent for white women and 13 percent for men of color.

"If you can't see other successful women who look like you, it's harder to relate and design a path of your own," says Shaunah Zimmerman, cofounder of Women Who Create, a community platform dedicated to fostering mentorship opportunities for women of color in the advertising industry.[104]

It stands to reason that, if Black women are one of few within their organization, they would have less access to women in leadership positions to develop

102   Girlboss. "Why Is It So Hard for Black Women to Find Mentors?" *Girlboss*, 2022. girlboss.com/blogs/read/2018-2-20-find-a-mentor-women-of-color.

103   Coury, Sarah, Jess Huang, Ankur Kumar, Sara Prince, Alexis Krivkovich, and Lareina Yee. "Women in the Workplace." McKinsey & Company, September 27, 2021. www.mckinsey.com/featured-insights/diversity-and-inclusion/women-in-the-workplace.

104   Girlboss, "Why Is It So Hard."

relationships that might lead to mentorship. Another question that immediately came to mind was the purpose of mentorship and whether there are quantifiable benefits that make pursuing one beneficial, especially given the dearth of potential mentors. In framing a complete understanding of the benefits of mentorship, I found that the first step was understanding exactly what a mentor is, what they can provide, and how this relationship differs from sponsorship.

A mentor is an individual who guides you through a specific career, goal, or even life. The mentor is often an individual who is more senior or advanced in your field and can provide you with advice and even connect you with others. The Black Girl Ventures Foundation (BGV) conducted an exclusive study[105] of a thousand working professionals to find out the impact mentorship has for women across races. BGV is an organization that addresses the unique challenges Black and Brown women face in accessing social and financial capital to grow their businesses.

The BGV study reveals that Black women experienced a 37.4 percent increase in average salary with mentorship. A mentor can do multiple things to help you get paid more, like helping you navigate your career route, provide opportunities, or connect with C-suite executives at companies you want to work for (if they are in that person's network). Having a mentor can be the difference between making $60,000 a year and making $82,000 a year.

So, an additional question many Black women ask is how mentorship differs from sponsorship and which one, if either, is more beneficial. Initially, I wasn't sure of the difference and thought the terminology to describe the roles was

105   James, Danielle. "Sista, Sista: How a Mentor Can Be the Key to Advancing Your Career." *Essence*, July 1, 2021. www.essence.com/news/money-career/mentor-key-career-advancement.

interchangeable. According to *Harvard Business Review*,[106] where mentorship focuses on help that a mentor can provide directly, such as guidance, advice, feedback on skills, and coaching, sponsorship entails externally facing support, such as advocacy, visibility, promotion, and connections.

Sponsorship can be understood as a form of intermediated impression management, where sponsors act as brand managers and publicists for their protégés. This work involves the management of others' views on the sponsored employee. Thus, the relationship at the heart of sponsorship is not between protégés and sponsors, as is often thought, but between sponsors and an audience—the people they hope to sway to the side of their protégés.

Rosalind Chow, an associate professor of organizational behavior and theory at Carnegie Mellon University, identifies[107] specific, concrete behaviors for sponsors to use to lift others. Tactics that are typically studied as forms of impression management can be translated into their sponsorship equivalents and have been coined by her as the ABCD of Sponsorship.

- **Amplifying**. Amplifying is the sponsorship equivalent of self-promotion. When sponsors amplify, they share protégés' accomplishments with others in a bid to create or increase an audience's positive impressions of them. By trumpeting the achievements of a protégé, sponsors avoid self-promotion and its potential pitfalls. This is particularly true for women, since female stereotypes dictate that they be self-effacing and humble.

- **Boosting**. Boosting is the sponsorship equivalent of self-assurance. When people put themselves forward for consideration for a position or opportunity, they're in effect making promises about their future performance. But most

---

106   Chow, Rosalind. "Don't Just Mentor Women and People of Color. Sponsor Them."
       Harvard Business Review, June 30, 2021. hbr.org/2021/06/dont-just-mentor-women-
       and-people-of-color-sponsor-them.

107   Chow, "Don't Just Mentor Women."

of us know that people are motivated to make themselves look good in these situations and may not present an accurate view of their own capabilities. These claims, then, may not hold as much weight as when they're made by a third party who presumably has a more objective opinion on how the protégé will perform. Here's where boosting comes into play: When sponsors boost their protégés, they stake some portion of their own reputation on an implicit guarantee about the protégé's future success. They underwrite it.

- **Connecting.** Connecting is the sponsorship equivalent of impression management through association—that is, claiming a relationship with a highly regarded individual or group so that some of the positive feeling others have toward them is transferred to the person claiming the association. This is often referred to as a "halo effect."

  When a high-status sponsor connects with a protégé, they claim the association, rather than the other way around. This enhances others' impression of the protégé because the sponsor has already been "vetted" by the community. Likewise, the protégé has passed the sponsor's standard for inclusion in their network. Connecting can also involve actively facilitating new relationships for protégés, giving them access to people they wouldn't otherwise be able to meet.

- **Defending.** Defending is the sponsorship equivalent of justifying or making personal excuses to change others' perceptions of them from negative to positive. In the same way, when a sponsor defends a protégé, they address an audience whose members dislike or dismiss the protégé and work to persuade them to change their opinion. Defending is, quite possibly, one of the most effective sponsorship tactics.[108]

Having a sponsor at work—someone who advocates for you—can mean the difference between getting a promotion and staying stagnant for years. Sponsorship

---

108   Chow, 2021

extends beyond mentorship and career advice. They call out your diligent work in meetings, mention your name in rooms you're not in, and can champion you when it comes time to hand out new opportunities.

According to joint research[109] by McKinsey & Company and LeanIn.org, Black women are much less likely than their colleagues to have a work sponsor. They're also less likely than other women to feel that promotions are fair and objective.

Given the tangible strategies that can be employed by sponsors and the genuine support offered by mentors, there's no doubt that having either or even both in your corner would be a benefit. However, based on the statistics of Black women represented in the workplace, particularly in leadership roles, Sherry Sims, founder of the Black Career Women's Network, noted[110] that among her clients, the most common impediment she's observed in Black women finding mentors was not knowing how to ask for support or where to look:

"80 percent of my clients prefer to be mentored by another African American woman that is currently working in a position they aspire to be in," she says. "Most often these women desire to be in a C-suite position and seek mentors currently in these roles. Unfortunately, they have limited access to these women due to a lack of representation in those roles."

When it comes to Black women and mentorship, a constant complaint is that there aren't "enough" Black women mentors, or the Black women at the top are "too burned out." BGV's blog manager and senior content writer, Frantzces Lys, admits,[111]

---

109   Ward, Marguerite. "The Checklist Black Women and Their Office Managers Can Use to Find Mentors Who Will Advocate for Them When It's Time for Promotions and Salary Raises." *Business Insider*, July 16, 2020. www.businessinsider.com/black-women-less-likely-to-have-sponsors-how-to-fix-2020-1.

110   Girlboss, "Why Is It So Hard."

111   Ward, "The Checklist Black Women and Their Office Managers Can Use."

"There's truth to that. There aren't enough Black women in leadership positions that can 'always' offer mentorship opportunities. Only 5.3 percent of Black women held leadership or professional positions in 2020."

With Black women facing disparities in the workplace, including microaggressions, lack of diversity, and being passed over for promotions, Lys hypothesizes the issue may be whether "[Black women] have the emotional bandwidth, while dealing with these barriers, to take on a mentee." Knowing this, it's no surprise the study reported that only 64 percent of the women who mentored Black women were other Black women, while 91.8 percent of white women mentor other white women.[112]

Before determining who might be a suitable mentor, a crucial prerequisite might be determining your goal. What do you need from a mentor? Is it career guidance and support? Maybe it's advice in a particular area, like marketing, social media, or entrepreneurship, within which she is a subject matter expert. With that being the case, most Black women I spoke with recommended having a whole team of mentors that could be called on. This is in contrast to depending on relationships cultivated with only one special person in your professional circle.

With this being the case, I found the most helpful strategy for me was to look outside of the traditional places. A huge part of that was expanding my horizons through networking and meeting other Black women. And this might not only happen in the workplace. Based on my own experiences, as well as the other women I spoke with, these relationships can be developed anywhere from mom and PTA groups to women we encounter at the park to women we attended high school or college with or who are members of our sororities or professional networking organizations. In addition, these women don't necessarily have to be women we meet in person. A great deal of virtual networking is taking place, especially since the pandemic. Being open to developing these relationships has been a big part of my ability to expand my networking

---

112   Ward, "The Checklist Black Women and Their Office Managers Can Use."

circle. This may happen within networking groups on professional platforms like LinkedIn, where I found that I was able to meet, collaborate with, and even enter business endeavors with other like-minded Black women.

With that being said, I also reframed my idea about what this type of relationship looked like and who I entered into it with. While traditional thinking might recommend seeking out the most high-profile mentor you can find, Shaunah Zimmerman, cofounder of Women Who Create, a community platform dedicated to fostering mentorship opportunities for women of color in the advertising industry, suggests looking at the people around you to start, rather than seeking out the big shots right out of the gate.

"...[T]he mentors women are finding are very high-level, and it's hard to foster a relationship when a hundred other people are also competing to get face time with them," Zimmerman says.[113] She recommends taking a deeper, broader look at your options: "Someone who's about to hit mid-level can be a great mentor. Even though they may not have [as much experience as a senior or executive-level employee], they may still have very powerful connections. If you really have a meaningful relationship with this mentor, it can lead to the senior-level introductions you want."

So, I began to reimagine what I thought a mentor's qualifications would be. That person didn't have to be a senior-level manager or older than me, which was the image I had in mind. I also thought the person who could serve as a mentor to me would need to be a seasoned veteran in their field, with management experience and decades of working in the C-suite. But to quite the contrary, I often found that the women I was able to learn from and who provided sound advice in my professional networking circle were often my age or even younger. Not all of them were more advanced in their careers. Sometimes they were new to a field but had learned quickly. This

---

113   Girlboss, "Why Is It So Hard."

i'm not yelling

was very common during the pandemic, as many Black women pivoted to new fields and even left corporate spaces to try their hands at entrepreneurship. And many of them were very quick studies who had been forced to learn a huge amount through trial and error during a short amount of time and unforeseeable challenges, as the whole world came to a grinding halt during a global shutdown. They may have just been more well-versed in a specific area like social media, entrepreneurship, or marketing. It was critical for me to look at the areas I needed to develop in and to align myself with women who had the same interests. And those relationships were often not even formed with people who worked in the same professional field that I was in. This is because I wanted to develop skills that were outside of the areas I already knew.

I also stopped looking at mentorship as though it was transactional and formal. Instead, I learned how to experience fluid, natural, and authentic relationships that are born from mutual trust and understanding. I found that seeking out commonalities and developing real friendships led to the mentoring goals and relationships I was searching for. Rather than asking someone to take me under their wing and teach me their ways, I started looking for ways to collaborate with other Black women who had similar values.

I sought out Black women with similar missions and values and looked for ways that we might team up to offer panel discussions or webinars on topics that we shared a passion for. When Black women reached out to me to appear on podcast discussions to promote my ideas, I was able to develop relationships based on shared admiration and trust. So, when it was time to approach women to appear on my podcast, I had already created a circle of women to speak with. In addition, I offered referrals from their own contacts for potential guests. The same has been true of potential business opportunities and even jobs. By looking at mentorship as relationship-building first and foremost, it no longer intimidates me as some mystical bond that I have to ask for. Rather, it was an authentic next step in our journey of getting to know each other.

From those natural give-and-take relationships, I formed bonds with women who naturally offered to help me, give me advice, or just listen to me because they saw I wasn't just there to "pick their brain" or take from them without attempting to give anything in return, although none of them ever asked me. But in the spirit of collaboration, I was always quick to ask high-level executive Black women I met to let me know if there was anything I could do for them. I wanted to show I was also interested in providing any support that they might need, even if I didn't necessarily have the level and range of skills that they did. It was amazing to see how many were surprised and grateful for the offer, even though the majority never took me up on it. I think showing that you are willing just goes a long way, especially with people who are used to being in high demand and having people ask them for favors.

This is another reason why creating and developing your own brand is so vital. Being someone who is inquisitive, actively working on their own career, and visibly networking also draws the attention of potential mentors. In becoming more intentional about my career goals, I demonstrated that I was motivated not only to learn but also to help others along the way; this made it easier for me to attract people who wanted to help me, offering advice or support. I think that sometimes people forget that even those in high-level positions at the top of their fields don't know everything. They are often inspired by people who are striving toward their goals and want to make an impact on the world. By actively networking and being aware of how to leverage your brand, you can attract the attention of people who can offer support and help when you least expect it.

One example that sticks out to me was my connection on social media with the CEO of a huge multi-million-dollar tech brand. He had been following my content and, after seeing him engage in my posts, I reached out to interview

i'm not yelling

him for a podcast I was hosting. He immediately shared how inspired he had been by my stand on social justice. He later pledged $25,000 to a scholarship fund in my name at Spelman College and even agreed to be a guest speaker for an MBA course I taught on anti-racism and diversity. These types of connections, and ultimately friendships and support, can come from people who want to be a part of your journey to success. They develop authentically and involve mutual respect and a genuine desire to help you.

This brings me to my next point, about choosing an appropriate mentor based on race and gender. Although most Black women surveyed preferred to be mentored by another Black woman, there are some benefits to having a mentor of another race or even gender—someone who acknowledges the privilege they have and are willing to leverage that privilege to help advance your career and support you in your goals. Sometimes these people can speak your name and amplify, uplift, and defend you in conversations behind closed doors that you don't have access to.

As an example, Jerry MacCleary, the former CEO of Covestro LLC, found himself constantly defending female employees and employees of color in evaluation meetings because he saw that white male managers were often criticizing their interpersonal styles as too outspoken or confrontational. MacCleary countered with personal examples that directly contradicted the other managers' claims. In this way, under his guidance, Covestro dramatically increased the diversity in its leadership ranks; at the time of his retirement, five of eleven top positions were held by women and people of color.[114]

---

114   Chow, "Don't Just Mentor Women."

Tonya Carruthers, chief human resources officer for PFF, shares[115] the same advice based on her own experience. "I'm really big on mentors, really big on advisors, and really big on advisors that don't look like me, because I learned that a long time ago by being at some of the larger companies and being in those rooms."

In my time on social media, I often connected with Black men who were in the C-suite of Fortune 500 companies, founders of companies, or media executives. Their ability to offer advice, guidance, or even encouragement and words of support was invaluable. Again, I learned that mentorship doesn't have to be an all-or-nothing endeavor, even though it may also be more structured and long-term with a plan and goal. I also learned that these offers to just help and lend a listening ear for specific questions or issues were also immensely helpful. Therefore, being open to networking, being visible as a thought leader, and developing a brand that can be leveraged are essential tools to attract the right circle of trusted mentors and sponsors.

According to the study by Black Girl Ventures,[116] women ultimately benefited from mentorship in several ways. Black women experienced a 37.4 percent increase in average salary with mentorship. More than 50 percent of women with mentors said they were very or extremely satisfied with their current jobs. Only 24.3 percent of women without mentors expressed a similar degree of satisfaction with work. Those who went without mentors were also most likely to express job dissatisfaction.

Perhaps this is the case because having a seasoned mentor allows for more networking, which opens the door to career moves that are the right match.

---

115   Carruthers, Tonya. "Strategic Career Moves for Ultimate Success." Interview by Elizabeth Leiba. *Black Power Moves, EBONY Covering Black America Podcast Network*, May 3, 2022. ebonypodcastnetwork.com/black-power-moves.

116   Black Girl Ventures Foundation. "Mentorship White Paper." Black Girl Ventures, 2023. www.blackgirlventures.org/mentorship.

Employees often walk away from a company due to dissatisfying salaries and a lack of growth opportunities. A mentor could help women negotiate their salaries ahead of time and make clear the desire to grow within an industry—before they settle for a career that doesn't meet their needs. And most women in the BGV study said their mentors were very or extremely helpful overall.

This is why the advice given by Oprah Winfrey is so salient in regard to the importance of a mentor in both career and professional development. This is also true regarding personal development. "A mentor is someone who allows you to see the hope inside yourself." They can see the potential in you, point out objectively how your growth and development can be nurtured, and inspire and motivate you to push forward. They see talents and ways for you to leverage these talents because mentors are often more proficient in skills that you want to master and have insights on how to get there. Because mentors have a unique place in your life, they also can view your journey from a position that encourages evolution and inspires you to make things happen.

A huge turning point in my professional career of advocating for social justice and change, using both social and mainstream media, was meeting a talented journalist named Ashanti Martin. After observing the uptick in activity on social media in the aftermath of George Floyd's murder in May of 2020, she noticed an even more interesting phenomenon on the LinkedIn platform primarily used for job searching, professional networking, and career advice. Black users of the platform were taking to their feeds to post about racial inequity, social justice, and a demand for change. I was one of them who Ashanti reached out to to interview for her story, which was published on the front page of the *New York Times* business section.

When she first reached out to me to interview me for the story, I was stunned. I wasn't even sure where she thought I might add value to the story. She explained that she had been following my posts on social media and thought my voice on the LinkedIn platform was powerful and unique. She cited several of my posts she had seen on the platform, including this one she captured in a screenshot on her phone:

 Elizabeth Leiba · 2nd   **+ Follow**   ···
Author, I'm Not Yelling. 📙 Pre-order on Amazon NOW! ·...
2yr · Edited · 🌐

NEWS FLASH 😮 Questioning my education credentials WILL NOT stop me from speaking out on SOCIAL INJUSTICE! ✊🏾

🎙️ I have a Bachelor's in journalism from University of Florida, an MBA with a concentration in Global Issues and additional graduate study in both Literature and Creative Writing.

🔎 Examining my professional experience WILL NOT stop me from speaking out about SYSTEMIC RACISM!

📷 I have worked in higher education for 20 years at more than a dozen college and universities, as an admissions counselor, a faculty member, and an online course designer. Check my LinkedIn. I have plenty of receipts! 🧾

✖️ Fact-checking my stats WILL NOT stop me from speaking out against RACIAL DISPARITIES, INEQUITY, DISCRIMINATION and the negative impacts on Black communities across America.

📰 I served as Newspaper Editor for the Seminole Tribune, the Official Newspaper for the Seminole Tribe of Florida on the Hollywood, FL Indian Reservation. I have a track record of being a voice for marginalized communities.

☑️ I am also well-versed in verifying my research and ensuring it can be found in multiple, credible sources. You won't find any FAKE NEWS in my posts no matter how much you dispute the veracity of my claims.

ANY QUESTIONS?

#blacklivesmatter #blackwomen #professionalwomen

https://www.linkedin.com/feed/update/urn:li:activity:6693923099290730496/

Her story featured me in the opening paragraphs. After speaking with her in our interview for more than an hour, I was able to see with more clarity the impact of what I was doing; my voice and presence on social media was resonating with others and changing the face of LinkedIn for good. Her validating my impact, putting it into context, and describing how it changed her engagement on the platform helped me to gain more confidence in what I was doing and why it was so meaningful. I continued to evolve in my advocacy work, with that interaction shaping my perspective of what it really meant to others. Ashanti became a close friend, mentor, and confidante, whom I trusted to be a listening ear and a sounding board as I continued my journey.

And that's another benefit of having trusted mentors. They see greatness in you. They help you to see yourself for who you are in the moment, as well as who you have the potential to be. They can be an advocate, a sponsor, an encourager, and a motivator. Even better are the sponsors who speak your name in rooms and leverage their influence to create opportunities for you that you didn't even know existed.

reflection questions ─────────────────

1. Have you ever had a mentor? If so, what are the qualities that he/she possessed that were beneficial in your personal and professional development?

2. If you have not had a mentor, why do you think this is the case?

3. What is the value of having a mentor at this point in your career? How might a mentor be able to help you achieve your goals and aspirations?

4. What qualities/characteristics are you looking for in a mentor?

5. What are some places where you might be able to find a mentor?

6. What strategies can you use to approach a mentor?

7. How might your personal brand contribute toward developing a relationship with a mentor?

8. What strategies can be used to create an authentic and genuine reciprocal relationship with a mentor?

9. What is the difference between a mentor and a sponsor?

10. What is the importance of having a sponsor? How might a sponsor contribute toward your personal and professional goals?

positive affirmations

1. "You can't know where you're going unless you know where you came from."   —Maya Angelou

1. "Am I good enough? Yes, I am."   —Michelle Obama

1. "Do the best you can until you know better. Then when you know better, do better."   —Maya Angelou

2. "I am no longer accepting the things I cannot change. I am changing the things I cannot accept."   —Angela Davis

3. "If they don't give you a seat at the table, bring a folding chair."
                                                            —Shirley Chisolm

4. "You've got to learn to leave the table when love's no longer being served"   —Nina Simone

5. "When someone shows you who they are, believe them the first time."   —Maya Angelou

6. "Breathe. Let go. And remind yourself that this very moment is the only one you know you have for sure." —Oprah Winfrey

7. "Let nothing dim the light that shines from within."
                                                            —Maya Angelou

8. "Once we recognize what it is we are feeling, once we recognize we can feel deeply, love deeply, can feel joy, then we will demand that all parts of our lives produce that kind of joy."
                                                            —Audre Lorde

In looking for mentors, think strategically about what you need to build the skill sets necessary to accomplish your personal and professional goals. Begin with the end in mind, and remember that you can have multiple mentors who can help you to meet your ultimate purpose. Also think about developing natural, mutually beneficial relationships in networking environments, both online and in person. Some of these may develop into mentorship opportunities. Also, think about what you bring to these interactions, so the potential mentor can gauge your skills and how they can add value. Ultimately, determine what your goal is. Having more people invested in your success will help you to step into your purpose.

Initially, I didn't have a sister circle or influential women I could call on for advice. So instead, I started making it a habit to quote women that I admired and draw on their strength, knowing everything they had to overcome. Their words gave me courage, and I found myself even using them in my everyday conversations, in a meeting, or during a speaking engagement. It helped me to remember I'm *never* alone because I'm standing on the shoulders of giants. These quotes became my affirmations for the types of mentors I knew I would attract to support me in my journey.

a seat at the table or building your own empire

"If they don't give you a seat at the table,

bring a folding chair."

—Shirley Chisolm

Once I got a seat at the table, I realized it was too small to hold all my ambitions. As I started to evaluate everything I had accomplished, people I had met, and experiences I had, it became apparent that I needn't be satisfied by tables that had already been built. My beloved soror of Delta Sigma Theta Sorority, Inc., Shirley Chisholm, advised, "If they don't give you a seat at the table, pull up a folding chair."

And while I agree with her wise counsel, as the first African American to run for a major party's nomination for president of the United States, in the 1972 US presidential election, I am also very much aware of the systemic barriers that exist preventing Black folk from even entering those rooms, let alone pulling up a folding chair at those tables. And not much has changed in the time since Shirley Chisolm's bid, making her also the first woman ever to run for the Democratic Party's presidential nomination.

We are standing outside a locked door with limited opportunity and sometimes no possibility of being allowed inside due to centuries of legislation, policy, and processes—all of which have effectively restricted our access to those spaces. And often, if we do receive access to those spaces, our ability to have a voice at those tables, to not be exposed to toxic environments that limit our effectiveness, to be retained to climb the corporate ladder to the ultimate prize of entrance into the golden doors of the C-suite, and to reach our ultimate potential in professional development, leadership, and financial rewards (compensating us for what we bring to the table) has been severely limited.

Kanika Tolver, author and CEO of Career Rehab, explains, "To understand what you're bringing to the table, you need to be understanding what they're bringing to the table for you is no longer the mindset. If you're trying to secure your seat, you're trying to be fed. When you get at that table, you're not trying to get the scraps. If you are feeling like you're not getting that, then you dump that job for another job. You go sit at another table where maybe you can feel like you're being fed properly, and it's to have the appropriate career growth that you want."[117]

My aspirations were so far beyond the table I knew I would never be satisfied there. A true lightbulb moment for me occurred when I realized that, not only was I worthy, I was more than worthy. I had been all along. It began to dawn on me that the tables where I had banged on the door, tentatively and quietly entered the room, had to justify and even validate my presence, before finally being permitted to speak my truth, had been too small for me.

It was empowering, exhilarating, and terrifying to realize that this validation I had been yearning for my entire life was something I didn't even desire anymore; my dreams, goals, and purpose were so much bigger. After stepping into my power and embracing it by walking in my truth, I began to see that the places I should inhabit were limitless, and that, by being satisfied to be "allowed" into spaces I had previously aspired to enter and even been grateful for the opportunity upon my arrival, I was doing myself a terrible disservice.

Since the COVID-19 pandemic began to sweep the globe in 2020, more and more focus is being placed on the importance of mental health, emotional well-being, and maintaining our own sense of integrity and empowerment. This surge in self-reflection has led Black folk, and particularly Black women, to wonder if the cost of being at those tables is worth it in the long run. Black adults in general (and Black women in particular) are more likely than white ones to report feeling sad and hopeless some of the time, according to the Substance Abuse and Mental Health Services Administration.[118]

---

117   Tolver, "Rebuilding Your Personal Brand."

118   Floyd, Lynya. 2020. "America Needs Black Women. We're Facing an Overwhelming Mental Health Crisis." *Prevention*. November 6, 2020. https://www.prevention.com/health/mental-health/a33686468/black-women-mental-health-crisis/.

In the workplace, Black women face a myriad of challenges, such as natural hair discrimination and microaggressions, that only intensify their lack of emotional well-being and contribute to mental health disorders. Because Black women experience both racial and gender bias, discrimination and the stress that comes with it are nearly constant, especially at work. This takes a toll on Black women's mental health. Multiple studies have shown that constant, long-term stress can increase the risk of developing mental health conditions—such as anxiety, depression, and even post-traumatic stress disorder. These social determinants don't just impact Black women's mental health. Racism and gender discrimination affect Black women on a biological level, aging them by at least 7.5 years and contributing to higher rates of stress-induced chronic illnesses such as diabetes and heart disease.[119]

Twenty-eight years ago, Kimberlé Crenshaw coined the term "intersectionality" in a paper for the University of Chicago Legal Forum to help explain the oppression of African American women. Crenshaw's then somewhat academic term is now at the forefront of national conversations about racial justice, identity politics, and policing—and over the years has helped shape legal discussions. A leading thinker and scholar in the field of critical race theory, Crenshaw, a professor at Columbia Law School, directs the Center for Intersectionality and Social Policy Studies and is a cofounder of the African American Policy Forum, a think tank.

Crenshaw wrote that traditional feminist ideas and antiracist policies exclude Black women because they face overlapping discrimination unique to them. "Because the intersectional experience is greater than the sum of racism and sexism, any analysis that does not take intersectionality into account cannot sufficiently address the particular manner in which Black women are subordinated," she wrote in the paper. "It's basically a lens, a prism, for

---

119   Colvin, Caroline. 2022. "Review of How One Collective Seeks to Protect Black Women at Work." HR Dive, February 10, 2022. https://www.hrdive.com/news/how-one-collective-seeks-to-protect-black-women-at-work/618641/.

seeing the way in which various forms of inequality often operate together and exacerbate each other. We tend to talk about race inequality as separate from inequality based on gender, class, sexuality, or immigrant status. What's often missing is how some people are subject to all of these, and the experience is not just the sum of its parts."[120]

She added, "When we talk about inequality, we are often talking about material differences in conditions of life. Take income inequality. Numerous statistics show that women still get paid less for the same work. That multiplies over a lifetime and means that the problem gets worse the older women get. There's also a term called the feminization of poverty, which speaks to all the ways that life circumstances—like child rearing, divorce, illness—impact women more profoundly. Across the social plane, from issue to issue, from institution to institution, you see women doing on average more poorly than men. [...] When you add on top of that other inequality-producing structures like race, you have a compounding. So, for example, data show that white women's median wealth is somewhere in the $40,000 range. Black women's is $100."

The juxtaposition between race and sex also seeks to create a lens through which to examine the duality of what it means to be Black and a woman, not just in our daily lives in reference to the criminal justice system, but also how that frames the way we navigate, perform, and are perceived in corporate America. More and more Black women are saying, "I can't feel like that anymore," and exiting corporate America in droves. While most of us are familiar with factors like the pay gap, the "Black Ceiling," and the often-discussed systemic barriers Black women face, few realize that for many, leaving the workplace has become a question of their mental and emotional survival.

---

120   Crenshaw, Kimberle. "Demarginalizing the Intersection of Race and Sex: A Black Feminist Critique of Antidiscrimination Doctrine, Feminist Theory and Antiracist Politics." *University of Chicago Legal Forum* 1989, no. 1 (December 7, 2015). chicagounbound.uchicago.edu/cgi/viewcontent.cgi?article=1052&context=uclf.

"It's a double bind. No matter what you do, you're damned. You stay silent. That's a problem. You speak out," says Tracy Laszloffy, PhD, from the Center for Relationship Healing.[121] "There's no way to be that is acceptable and that you will be validated and rewarded for. That is the nature of oppression. There is no option you can choose that is considered acceptable. That is the dilemma," she adds—a dilemma Dr. Laszloffy says is forcing Black women to choose between unbearable psychological and emotional stress and leaving corporate cultures to create their own work environment.

According to Lean In's report on the State of Black Women in Corporate America,[122] only about a third of Black women surveyed said their manager gives them the opportunity to manage people and projects, compared to 39 percent of Latinas, 40 percent of Asian women and 43 percent of white women, who said their managers give them increased opportunities for leadership. On average, Black women in the US are also paid 36 percent less than white men and 20 percent less than white women. The wage gap for Black women means they make a lower wage on average than white men and white women in similar positions.[123]

And the truth remains that Black women are vastly underrepresented in leadership positions due to the continued barriers they face: Only 4.4 percent of Black women are in management positions and only 1.4 percent hold C-suite positions, despite being 7.4 percent of the US population. Even with an increased focus on diversity, equity, and inclusion within companies, the daily experience

---

121   Tisdale, Stacey. "[Diversity & Inclusion - Mental Health] Why Black Women Are Really Abandoning Corporate America." *Wealth Wednesdays*, 2021. www.teamwealthwednesdays.com/blog/diversity-amp-inclusion-mental-health-why-black-women-are-really-abandoning-corporate-america.

122   "The State of Black Women in Corporate America." *Lean In*, 2022. leanin.org/research/state-of-black-women-in-corporate-america.

123   Corbett, Holly. "How to Be an Ally for Black Women in the Workplace." *Forbes*, 2022. www.forbes.com/sites/hollycorbett/2022/02/22/how-to-be-an-ally-for-black-women-in-the-workplace/?sh=1e9bb5213123.

of Black women in the workplace hasn't improved in the last few years. Black women are almost twice as likely as women overall to say that they can't bring their whole selves to work. In addition, they are more than 1.5 times as likely to say they don't have strong allies, according to the Women in the Workplace 2021 report.[124]

Despite all these challenges, I must acknowledge that we do need those powerful, outspoken voices to ascend to leadership roles. These voices need to champion the cause for greater equity for Black folk and particularly Black women. But being realistic about the movement for change in what tangible actions are necessary to create meaningful and measurable traction in these initiatives is also very necessary. According to a new survey titled "Black Women Thriving,"[125] from Every Level Leadership, a consulting firm dedicated to helping organizations create inclusive environments, companies don't have adequate policies to protect and promote Black women, and it's leading them to report lower job satisfaction, increased challenges to career mobility, and a higher likelihood of quitting for a different job.

According to the survey of 1,431 Black women, 75 percent believe their organization does not take full advantage of their skills. Plus, 63 percent report they don't see a path to advance their career within their current organization. As a result, 71 percent say they'd quit for a new job to get a pay raise or promotion. Survey respondents also called attention to how non-inclusive workplaces impact their mental health. While most Black women say they feel valued for their contributions at work and they have the freedom to make their own decisions, 88 percent experience burnout on the job sometimes, often or always, due to the pressures of performing in non-supportive environments.

---

124   Corbett, "How to Be an Ally."

125   Jackson, Ashton. 2022. "Black Women Are in 'Survival Mode' at Work—and Company Diversity Efforts 'Fall Short.'" CNBC. July 1, 2022. https://www.cnbc.com/2022/07/01/company-diversity-efforts-to-support-black-women-fall-short.html.

Rather than feeling a sense of dread, these survey results give me a sense of clarity and understanding that we, as Black women, had not had access to. We've always been told to expect things to be twice as hard when we enter predominantly white spaces. But we were also told that if we worked hard and had the education and experience, our efforts would pay off. The vast amount of research, studies, and attention focused on the experiences of Black folk, particularly Black women, in the past two years has shown that this advice has not been validated by our real-life experiences in the workplace. And if anything, most of us have begun to have an even more astonishing understanding that it's not just us. It's easy to think that's the case when we're one of a handful of people who look like us. Our experiences have been shared in mainstream media, in research and survey results, and even in social media. The playing field isn't leveled. It hasn't been for a very long time. It's not because we're not qualified or worthy. In fact, we're more than worthy.

In my own journey, I spent most of my professional career dreaming about rising to the C-suite and doing everything I could to show I had the skills, dedication, and motivation to be there. But after almost twenty years working in my field, when I was eventually promoted, I found myself increasingly dissatisfied. It was like the moment in The Wizard of Oz when Dorothy finally peeked behind the curtain: I was totally disappointed by what I witnessed. The endless meetings, mediocrity, and ineptitude were initially surprising but also enlightening. I finally had a seat at the table. However, I found that, not only was I more qualified than many of the people seated there, my voice was also being muffled. I was constantly having to validate my presence and prove I was qualified. That was exhausting! Then there was navigating microaggressions and dealing with the politics of corporate leadership. The constant anxiety and feeling that there was something more in store for me were additional indicators that I still had not reached my ultimate potential. After using my arrival here as the sign that I had made it, I received an awareness that seemed almost intuitive based on my experiences. This wasn't the final place I was supposed to be, and there was so much more the world had to offer and that I needed to give in return.

Increasingly, especially since the pandemic, Black women are prioritizing our health and well-being where it comes to the workplace. The Center for Public Integrity says that since September, 181,000 Black women have left the workforce, even as the labor force participation rate of women in all other racial groups has increased. Experts also explain it's likely that Black women are refusing to return to certain low-paying jobs, which put them and their families at risk of contracting COVID-19 while not offering any paid sick days or health insurance.[126] In addition to focusing on practical needs, a growing number of us are focusing on our own wants and desires. According to Barron's, many Black women are racing to become entrepreneurs. Working within systems where we are underpaid and feel undervalued, it is no surprise why. For many of us, entrepreneurship is the only way to enjoy a taste of freedom.

Businesses owned by Black women represented the highest rate of growth in recent years, according to a report commissioned by American Express.[127] From 2014 to 2019, the number of businesses owned by Black women grew by 50 percent, outpacing women-owned businesses overall, which grew by 21 percent. The report also found that three factors drove the latest rise in women-owned businesses: opportunity, flexibility, and necessity. For many Black women, starting a business, or even looking at the possibility of multiple streams of income by incorporating side hustles alongside our primary career, offers the possibility of freedom, independence, and a sense of liberation from the minefield of the predominantly white corporate spaces we have previously navigated and had been taught to believe were the only places we could thrive.

---

126   Campbell, Alexia Fernández. "Black Women Are Still Dropping Out of the Workforce. Here's Why." Center for Public Integrity, December 17, 2021. publicintegrity.org/inside-publici/newsletters/watchdog-newsletter/black-women-jobs-dropping-out-of-workforce.

127   Bradley, Jarie A., and Kristina C. Dove. 2021. "Review of Why Black Women Are Leaving the Workforce." Barron's, June 18, 2021. https://www.barrons.com/articles/why-black-women-are-leaving-the-workforce-51623962131.

My first experience with the importance of multiple streams of income in addition to my primary job came after being laid off three times in three years. I had transitioned from working in admissions in higher education to working in phone sales in healthcare, then to the mortgage business. My final stop before returning to higher education was a position as the editor of a tribal newspaper on the Seminole Tribe's reservation. It was there that I saw the true nature of what it means to "build your own table." From the schools to the casinos to every function of tribal government, everything was designed to focus on the needs and interests of the tribal members, even monthly dividend checks that were large enough to live on, giving most members of the Tribe the option not to work. And for those who applied for open positions, tribal member hiring preferences were strictly enforced.

As a brown person and student of history, although I was not included in these preferences in any way, learning how South Florida's ancient Native American communities evolved to develop alliances with African American maroons, mostly self-emancipated former slaves from the South's Low Country and some free Blacks from the Spanish period of rule, was fascinating.[128] These people became known as Black Seminoles. During the Seminole Wars against the United States in the nineteenth century, most Seminole and Black Seminole were forced by the US to relocate west of the Mississippi River to Indian territory. A smaller group—possibly fewer than five hundred—refused to leave Florida and moved deep into the Everglades, where they avoided settlers and thrived in semi-isolation.[129] In 1975, the Tribe established tax-free smoke shops and a high-stakes bingo operation that became one of the first tribal gaming endeavors in the United States. These ventures, particularly the gaming operation, have generated

---

128   Frank, Andrew K. 2018. *Before the Pioneers: Indians, Settlers, Slaves, and the Founding of Miami.*

129   Mahon, John K. 2017. *History of the Second Seminole War, 1835-1842. Florida and the Caribbean Open.*

significant revenues for education, welfare, and economic development. A 2005 tribal audit said it took in $1.1 billion in revenues that year.[130]

Although I was laid off from my position working for the Seminole Tribe, the experience did bring clarity that I could not rely on any one source of income; I needed to be strategic in ensuring that I wouldn't fall victim to being financially impacted by workplace politics as I had been working for the Tribe. At that point, I began to consider the idea of getting back into higher education, but this time as a faculty member. It would allow me to supplement my full-time job by teaching college-level writing and literature in the evenings. As a single mom at the time, the idea of being able to teach classes online with a young child at home was also extremely attractive. And being able to work as an adjunct faculty member at a few different colleges and universities gave me an additional income that was almost the equivalent of my full-time job. It was then that I embraced the idea of always having at least one side hustle in addition to my main gig. In the last couple of years, since the pandemic began, my gigs have evolved from teaching college courses to developing and offering my own online courses for students of Black history and culture, as well as speaking engagements and sponsorship opportunities leveraging my experience and expertise.

Looking at the evolution of my attitude toward work and my engagement with my role in the workplace, there's been a period of preparation, growth, and flight—not unlike the passage from childhood to adulthood, from a cocoon to a butterfly, or any other time of transformation. During all my negative experiences with environments where I didn't feel as though I could bring my full and authentic self to work, I contended with microaggressions and questioned my own worth, while struggling to find my voice and understand its power. Rather than destroying me, those situations led to reflection; they opened a world of possibility where those pervasive and nagging doubts were not a part

---

130   Kestin, Sally. "The Seminole Tribe Is Suddenly Wealthy, but Little Oversight Means Potential Abuses." *Sun Sentinel*, 2013. www.sun-sentinel.com/news/sfl-semday1newsbnov25-story.html.

of my reality. By leaning into that hope, I was able to quiet that fear and enter a period of rapid growth. This was fueled by a sense that not only was I worthy in every single space I inhabited, but I was also so much more than worthy.

Grasping this new and improved reality, I began to embrace the idea that anything was possible. Spurred by the movement that I witnessed after the murder of George Floyd, it became evident that many of us were navigating spaces with the exact same feelings. We knew that our lack of feeling accepted, lack of belonging, being questioned, and not being valued were not just figments of our imagination. As we began to lift our voices in shared pain and confusion, we understood more than anything that none of this was our fault. The next question was what to do about it. For many of us, this new knowledge brought a sense of comfort: we could use our acceptance of this reality to be more intentional in how we navigate white spaces. No longer were we tentative and fearful. More than anything, we now had confidence in basing our attitudes on facts and statistics rather than emotions.

Some of us took this knowledge a step further to become outspoken advocates in mainstream and social media for equity and change. But even though this was the direction I pursued, I also have an immense amount of respect for the frontline leaders who work in the diversity, equity, and inclusion space in corporate America, as well as those who remain committed to pursuing their dreams in whatever field is most meaningful for them. Although there is tremendous value in any of these endeavors, one more benefit of the upheaval, both socially and economically, during the pandemic and in the months following the murder of George Floyd was the idea that a revolution doesn't just occur on the frontlines of protest. Revolution can also take place internally. For many of us, that growth in perspective led to flight. Some of us soared in our careers with this newfound knowledge. Many of us also transcended into spaces we had never previously imagined, perhaps outside the realms of places we had previously inhabited, and beyond even our own wildest dreams. In part because we became more open, the universe itself was able to open and succumb to our understanding: despite our desire to change, we refused to be limited. If that meant creating our own tables, then so be it.

With this being the case, it's wise to lean into the power of your own voice and experience, leveraging them for the most advantageous opportunities possible, whether at work or independently in business or both. Being open to using my voice to confidently express the level of my knowledge and abilities became the cornerstone of my personal brand. I became known for speaking my truth, no matter the consequences. But everyone's brand is different, depending on their area of expertise. Focusing on how to use that love and passion, while standing in truth and confidence, is the key not only to understanding your "why," but also to taking advantage of those opportunities as well as creating your own if or when you're ready.

I've gotten some amazing advice from the Black women I've met along my own journey of self-discovery. From Madison Butler, founder of Rage to Rainbows and Black Speakers Collective, I received probably the deepest insight about navigating work as a Black woman in predominantly white spaces. I asked her about the conflict that Black folk tend to feel when we are navigating those spaces. There is a sense that, although we have been conditioned to pursue success and leadership roles within these organizations, sometimes these spaces are not the most healthy for our mental and emotional well-being. As a DEI consultant, it's a phenomenon she often contends with in determining which clients to work with in meaningful ways.

"I'm a really big advocate for not working with people, and I'm really open when I have these initial exploratory calls," she said.[131] "I may not be the right person for you and here are the reasons why. And I'm very up from the jump in here's what you're going to get from me, and it's not going to be warm and fluffy and

131   Butler, Madison. "Spicy Hot Takes and Scorching Hot Tea." Interview by Elizabeth Leiba. *Black Power Moves, EBONY Covering Black America Podcast Network,* January 12, 2022. ebonypodcastnetwork.com/black-power-moves.

like, 'Let's slap a DEI badge on you when we've done the work.' This work is going to be hard. I'm going to make you uncomfortable. Every workshop I start with, 'You're going to feel uncomfortable, and encourage you to feel that. I encourage you to feel that right now because if we don't feel that then, we don't move things along.' So, I've definitely had to break up with clients who I realize weren't a match for me because they were asking me to do that."

She explained further, "I had a client who [said], 'We really want to focus on your Black identity. But if you could just not be so queer, that would be great!' Well, that's not really how it works. It's not like the grocery store. You don't get to pick and choose which ingredients you want. If you want that, you can go find it. But it's going to be with someone else. We see that, whether it's consulting or speaking or your full-time job, I think we've all experienced this space and mindset of, 'Do I belong here?' And I think what we really have to change the narrative for ourselves, like, 'Does this space deserve me?' And it took me a really long time to start thinking like that."

Hearing that one question posed in such an eloquent and self-reflective way changed how I viewed each predominantly white professional space I inhabited. Rather than looking at a place as somewhere I aspired to be, I focused on the positive benefits, experience, and knowledge I was bringing when I graced the space with my presence. For some of us, this mind shift may seem cocky. The idea of asking if a place deserves us may fly in the face of everything we have been taught. We have always been told to work twice as hard in the hopes that our contributions might be recognized; however, we must remember that by the very act of entering a space, we've already proven the value we add. By facing each challenge from a position of power and confidence, we've already defeated any potential imposter syndrome because we've already established what we bring to the table. It's now the job of those sitting at the table to recognize the value and not our job to justify our presence. And if they don't recognize our value, it's no longer our responsibility to prove it. We can decide not to be there, rather than fighting to convince those in the majority to acknowledge it.

Another piece of amazing advice came from Kanika Tolver, career coach and author of *Career Rehab*. Her recommendation is to look at your job as a "friend with benefits rather than a relationship."[132] Many of us have been conditioned to think of each employment opportunity as a commitment, rather than taking each engagement at face value. We should be interviewing each hiring manager as they are interviewing us. We should be asking ourselves whether this space will value our contributions. What does the environment look like there? This can be ascertained by browsing resources like Glassdoor, following current employees on social media, and even doing research on the organization by researching its social media presence and website. What is the company's commitment to diversity, equity, and inclusion? What does the C-suite look like? What do current employees have to say about the organization?

Even after we've done our due diligence and entered that space, we should go into it with the knowledge that, if the environment is not conducive to our professional and personal development, financial growth and goals, and overall desires, then we're not obligated to be there. Oftentimes, like any "relationship" rather than a "friends with benefits" situation, we spend far too much time investing in a situation that is toxic, knowing that our needs won't be met in that environment. Focusing on what we can learn rather than attempting to change the environment is another recommendation. I remember when Nikole Hannah Jones resigned from the University of North Carolina after not receiving a tenured professorship. After receiving a Pulitzer Prize for her highly regarded *New York Times* 1619 project and deciding to take a teaching position at Howard University, she observed that it was not her job to "heal" UNC. And like her, many of us must come to terms with that harsh truth. It's not our job to heal each predominantly white space we enter. Sometimes we need to focus on our own healing and emotional well-being because no one can pour from an empty cup. If our own cup is full, we will be less likely to stay in places that do not keep us fulfilled.

---

132   Tolver, "Rebuilding Your Personal Brand."

And so, my own journey of settling for less after twenty years in higher education, then seeing the world of opportunity that began to open when I became more confident in the power of my voice, began to explore the impact of my brand, and started networking and taking advantage of possibilities beyond my current circumstances, ended just like that. The realization that not only was I worthy at these tables, but that I was more than worthy. A priceless lesson I learned was that my voice had an impact not only at these tables but far beyond.

I learned the importance of leveraging your voice and harnessing the power of your story to create opportunity. It's essential for personal, professional, and entrepreneurial success to leave your options open to all possibilities. Probably the most valuable lesson I learned was not to be afraid to leave places where you are not valued or appreciated. Once I had a seat at the table, the realization that I had outgrown that space, and that I needed to expand my world to take advantage of all the possibilities, was life-changing. It led to being a social media influencer, being interviewed by national publications, having a podcast on a major podcast network, and having the opportunity to write this book that you're reading right now. None of this would have been possible if I had resigned myself only to the tables where I had been "allowed" to pull up a folding chair. Once I looked outside of these spaces, I found that the tables I had built for myself were so much more welcoming and, overall, more beneficial in all the ways that I needed and wanted.

Never be afraid to leave a table when there is no longer an opportunity that fits your amazing abilities. Singer, songwriter, pianist, and civil rights activist Nina Simone famously said, "You've got to learn to leave the table when love's no longer being served." Many of us need to remind ourselves that we are not required to remain in spaces that are unhealthy physically, mentally, and emotionally. This applies to both our personal and professional journeys. We should recognize these places for what they are. Very often these spaces are stops along our journey, and not our goal. And we shouldn't try to force these environments to provide what we need when they don't have the capacity to do so in a meaningful way. Being there may provide us with knowledge, experience, or the connections that we need to fulfill our dreams; these spaces, however, are rarely where we will step into our purpose. And often that purpose is closely aligned with our passion. Stepping into that truth with our most authentic self is typically where we will find true happiness. That true happiness lies within us and does not need external validation. That happiness is our truth, and we have the power to use our voices to tell our own stories that encompass that truth. Fulfillment comes from stepping into that truth and walking to the head of the table in whatever capacity fits our needs—knowing that love will be served at the table every single day we sit there.

reflection questions

1. What are your professional goals? Are you on track to meet your goals in the next six months? One year? Five years?

2. What are your financial goals?

3. What are your personal goals?

4. What will it take to get to the goals you have set for yourself?

5. What strategies or tools can you implement to help accomplish your goals?

6. What does your table look like right now? Are you happy, content, satisfied there? If not, why?

7. What can you do to improve your current table, and how will these improvements help move you closer to the professional, financial, and personal goals you have set?

8. What would your ideal table look like? Who would be sitting there? What would your role look like at the head of this table?

9. What steps would you need to take to manifest this table in the next six months? One year? Five years?

10. What is the biggest takeaway that you have learned in this journey of self-reflection? What is one step you can take today to help manifest your goals?

positive affirmations ────────────

1. I step into greatness every day.

2. I am confident.

3. I walk in my truth.

4. I am powerful.

5. I am beautiful.

6. I know my worth.

7. I speak my mind.

8. I am intelligent.

9. I am proud.

10. I am a queen.

conclusion

I know the best is yet to come for me, and I'm embracing each opportunity that comes my way. You can do the same thing. It's a matter of taking the first step. What is your why? How does it tie into your personal narrative, and how can you use your voice to articulate that story? Once you've harnessed the strength in your story, you will be unstoppable.

If there's one lesson I've learned, a mantra I believe in, and an affirmation I repeat to myself daily, it's that my voice is power. My voice is worthy. My voice is authentic. My voice is true. And I will never fail to recognize how critical it is to step into that reality every day as I navigate the world around me.

Don't let anyone tell you that you're yelling. You're not. You are standing in your truth and authentic power, using your voice to reflect all that you were, all that you are, and all that you will be. There is power in your voice. It deserves to be heard. Don't be scared to use it!

But before you begin to use your voice, you must start by asking yourself some really challenging questions. The answers to these questions will create the framework for why you need to use your voice and why. They will also help you focus on your purpose when you feel discouraged. And trust me, there will be times when you want to give up. Being clear in your why will keep you focused. Who you are as a person is central to what your purpose really is. Why were you put on this earth? What do you hope to accomplish while you are here, and what is it about who you are at your core that makes you so special?

The answers to these questions are what make your voice so compelling that it deserves and absolutely needs to be heard. Who are you? How do you feel, and how do you act when you are at your most comfortable and feeling like your most authentic self? What does that look like to you? How does that align with who you are today as you navigate predominantly white spaces in the world? By finding a way to align who you are at your most raw, real, and authentic with how you operate and present yourself in every other space, you are not only challenging societal norms, but you are also releasing yourself from the shackles of societal expectations that have told you who you really are is not good enough. Start there. Look in the mirror and ask yourself: Who am I?

Understanding who you are helps to nurture that desire inside to use that knowledge for internal and external growth and change. How do you use your own personal "why" to give you the strength to use your voice in meaningful ways?

Begin to think about the small ways that you can tell your story and create a narrative for yourself that is accurate, authentic, and meaningful. You may start by speaking up in a meeting where you might otherwise have been quiet. As you gain more confidence, think about ways that you can continue to leverage your voice. Have you been contemplating asking for a raise or promotion but postponed having that conversation with your boss? Craft a story that explains why you deserve that promotion. That process can be intimidating, but often if we wait for those opportunities to come to us, they will never be forthcoming. Creating a narrative of competence and excellence puts us in line for opportunities and empowers us. Waiting for someone to recognize our greatness can lead to a waiting game that we may never win.

Another consideration is thinking about how to leverage your voice. I was able to do that using social media. The beautiful thing about social media is that it gives you the ability to tell your story quickly, consistently, and authentically in any way you want. You can also scale your voice in a way that allows you not only to reach people all over the world, but also to create a brand that expands outside the physical workplace and establishes you as a subject matter expert in your field. Social media can be as simple as a blog, podcast, YouTube channel, or any other medium where you can speak your truth. Using this as a strategy for empowering your voice also creates a marketing tool for you to take advantage of additional opportunities, such as consulting within your field. It might present other opportunities that you never thought of.

If in considering how you can use the power of your voice, you start second-guessing your ability, asking yourself why people should listen to you or whether you have something meaningful that people need to hear, ask yourself why. Do you think you might be suffering from imposter syndrome? And if you do, ask yourself why. I recently stopped embracing this definition for what I was feeling because I feel that it pathologizes and creates a dichotomy that I'm uncomfortable with. As a young child, I never felt "imposter syndrome." Growing up in a predominantly Black neighborhood and attending a predominantly Black middle school and high school, I never felt like I wasn't capable or competent. In fact, I was told by my parents, Black teachers, administrators, mentors, and community leaders that I could accomplish any- and everything. I was encouraged to step into my greatness and always told that I was a queen descended from the African continent that was the cradle of civilization.

It wasn't until I began to navigate predominantly white spaces, beginning in college that I felt like I wasn't good enough. The accomplishments that had won me praise, support, and admiration in my previous environment were met with indifference and disdain. I was told that I had to prove myself if I wanted to show that I was worthy. And it was then that I started to second-guess and doubt almost every academic and professional decision that I made. I didn't have the same confidence or swag that I did in my younger years. I was hesitant, cautious, and afraid of making mistakes, forgetting that mistakes are a part of growth. Instead, I looked at a mistake as utter failure and walked on eggshells hoping to avoid them.

I consider this imposter treatment. We don't have a syndrome that makes us feel that we're less than worthy. We are treated as such and internalize having to work twice as hard to get the same promotion that comes easily to others who may be less qualified; we are still being passed over for opportunities we know we deserve. Often the only difference from our competitors is the color of our skin. Know this: You are worthy and deserve to be in every space you inhabit.

In embracing the idea that I deserved to be in each and every space I inhabit, I also decided to discard the exhausting and self-defeating practice of code-switching. To be myself, step into every space with the full knowledge that I belong there, and to speak my truth in every way, I had to embrace the authentic way I showed up. That relates to the way we speak, dress, and move. It's in the way we wear our hair. It's in our natural way of being. There is absolutely nothing unprofessional about our Blackness. And I enter every space with the intent to be myself in every way. I am unapologetically me. I'm unapologetically dope. I refuse to deviate from that stance, and I encourage you to do the same!

Embrace every opportunity that comes your way. If opportunities are not presented in a reasonable amount of time, never be afraid to step away from the table. We are not required to stay in spaces where we are not appreciated, nurtured, inspired, and compensated fairly. And if our needs are not being met, we can move on to another table, or build our own table.

How do you do that? Develop a community of support. This can be done both in person and online. Seek out mentorship from those willing to encourage you and provide the resources needed. Love yourself first and foremost. Don't wait for others to do it for you. Step into the power of your own greatness, your own voice, and your own power. Remember, you're not yelling. You're quietly speaking the truth.

about the author

Elizabeth Leiba is a writer, college professor, and advocate for Black businesswomen. She has over 100,000 followers on LinkedIn who range in age, race, background, and location, and are primarily located in the US, Canada, and the UK.

Her passion for Black history changed her life and catapulted her into a fulfilling line of work as a powerful advocate of social justice and equity for Black women, especially Black businesswomen. Elizabeth strives to create resources which support, empower, and amplify Black businesswomen and their businesses.

She was featured in the 2020 *New York Times* article, "Black LinkedIn Is Thriving. Does LinkedIn Have a Problem With That?," which highlighted her social justice advocacy work. The response to this article spurred her to launch her online, accessible e-learning platform, Black History & Culture Academy, the stunning educational resource which earned her the recognition of a LinkedIn Top Voice in Education in 2020.

She is also the host of *Black Power Moves*, a podcast on the Ebony Covering Black America Podcast Network, and is a published writer. Her most recent writing includes an op-ed piece on racial profiling for CNN, which had more than two million views on their news website.

In early 2022, Elizabeth launched her website directory, Black Women Handle Business, which is the premier website for Black women entrepreneurs and professionals to network, collaborate, and share resources.

Mango Publishing, established in 2014, publishes an eclectic list of books by diverse authors—both new and established voices—on topics ranging from business, personal growth, women's empowerment, LGBTQ studies, health, and spirituality to history, popular culture, time management, decluttering, lifestyle, mental wellness, aging, and sustainable living. We were recently named 2019 *and* 2020's #1 fastest growing independent publisher by *Publishers Weekly*. Our success is driven by our main goal, which is to publish high quality books that will entertain readers as well as make a positive difference in their lives.

Our readers are our most important resource; we value your input, suggestions, and ideas. We'd love to hear from you—after all, we are publishing books for you!

Please stay in touch with us and follow us at:

Facebook: Mango Publishing
Twitter: @MangoPublishing
Instagram: @MangoPublishing
LinkedIn: Mango Publishing
Pinterest: Mango Publishing
Newsletter: mangopublishinggroup.com/newsletter

Join us on Mango's journey to reinvent publishing, one book at a time.

CPSIA information can be obtained
at www.ICGtesting.com
Printed in the USA
JSHW032142090423
40059JS00006B/18